PHILIP G. PALUMBO, CFP®

MAKE WORK OPTIONAL

Achieve Financial Peace of Mind

Published by **2MARKET MEDIA** with Philip G. Palumbo, CFP®

ISBN 979 8 399 92984 2

To my wife, my best friend and biggest fan, thank you.

*To my three sons, dream big, work hard, and you
will achieve anything you put your mind to!*

CONTENTS

FOREWORD

To achieve true peace of mind in your financial life, I believe it is essential to build, maintain and execute a comprehensive wealth management plan, one tied directly to helping you achieve your life objectives. In doing so, many investors, regardless of initial wealth, have the potential to accelerate the point at which work becomes optional for them.

I sincerely hope this book can serve to further educate and raise the awareness of *all* investors to *demand* from their financial advisors the fully comprehensive, disciplined wealth management approach Phil espouses in this book. Sadly, many are not getting this benefit today.

The book highlights anecdotes from Phil's twenty-two years on the front lines in some of the largest wealth management firms, outlining how he sought out and incorporated best practices into his business. It also provides an outline of his approach to managing his client's assets, using lessons learned from Warren Buffett and Ray Dalio. These lessons are highlighted in one of Phil's many educational webinars, *Invest Like the Best*. The book also includes insight into his entrepreneurial desire to launch his own firm, offering him the freedom to deliver the best wealth management service for his clients.

It was always Phil's vision to serve as an investor's "personal chief financial officer", and one that I shared as well. That, along with his passion for excellence in wealth management, drove me to accept the role as his Senior Advisor prior to him launching his own firm in early 2020. In the face of COVID, Phil launched Palumbo Wealth Management (PWM) to broadly share his highly disciplined and truly comprehensive approach to wealth management with the world. You'll see Phil's attention to discipline in his 5-step consultative process, religiously followed when initiating a client relationship, and the crafting of his own "wealth management formula" with acronyms outlining the key components.

It was impressive to watch most of his clients follow Phil to his new firm in the midst of the COVID market meltdown, and I was excited to become one of his first new clients.

I have always seen the potential disruptive opportunity in wealth management, and I enjoy disruptive challenges that draw me in. In my over 40 years in financial services across both the "institutional and retail" sides of the business, I have remained disappointed with the inconsistent level of the adoption of best practices across the wealth management field. All investors, regardless of asset size, should be able to benefit from a disciplined investment approach and comprehensive financial planning under the direction of a wealth manager that serves as a true fiduciary.

An example of this inconsistency can be seen in *JD Power's 2022 U.S. Full-Service Investor Satisfaction Study*, which surveyed over 4,000 investors of comprehensive wealth management firms, showing that ***only 14% of those investors surveyed are receiving the full comprehensive financial service advice that is offered by these firms.*** I believe, as Phil does, that all investors deserve the same comprehensive approach, and the Study indicates that they are not benefitting, even with the largest of firms and the wealthiest of investors.

Growing up in a middle-class lifestyle, Phil discloses his motivation to target wealth management as his career. A fan of the former *Wall Street Week* television show, hosted by the late Louis Rukeyser, Phil learned in his childhood about the value of hard work and the importance of understanding the financial world. This upbringing, along with his powerful work ethic, has driven him to build the best wealth management practice possible, serving as a fiduciary and placing his clients' interests first. Now with his name on the door, he is truly free to incorporate best practices for the firm's clients.

Phil's dedication to ongoing education and continually refining his firm's portfolio approach has allowed him to further diversify the client portfolios, with the careful and measured addition of alternatives. Additionally, Phil leads the PWM team, including Doug Augenthaler, another 40+ year veteran of Wall Street, continually maintaining an active research agenda, seeking out portfolios and investment strategies with more attractive risk-adjusted returns.

Phil understands the ideal wealth management practice incorporates time-tested and dedicated research, a disciplined investment approach consistently applied, with an eye toward value across all investments, and all wrapped up within a comprehensive financial plan.

Thank you, Phil, for your true tireless dedication to helping *all* investors *Make Work Optional*!

William Gordon

Senior Advisor, Palumbo Wealth Management

Founder, Peconic Bay Partners, LLC

Past Co-Founder, Dix Hills Partners, LLC

INTRODUCTION

WHAT IF?

What if you could take the worry out of money? How would you feel? How would your life be different, day in, day out, year after year?

And work? Do you stay at your job or profession out of love for it? Or are you worried you won't have enough money to maintain your lifestyle—or maybe any lifestyle? Are you wondering about when you can "afford to" retire? Are you wondering if you even want to retire?

Well, what if you could make work truly optional? What if you could save and invest strategically, efficiently, and diligently throughout your prime working years, so that walking away from work—on your own terms—became a viable option? How would you feel? And how would your life, your health, your outlook be different? Would it be fuller? More meaningful? More satisfying? Better?

Think about it. As a concept, retirement is old-school—and not in a good way. It's outdated. You shouldn't be forced into a binary decision: To work or to retire? To be or not to be? What if I could tell you—for real—that instead of working and investing and saving for retirement, you could be working and investing and saving to make work optional?

So many people, maybe even most of us, live each day worrying about money. They end up deprived of their best possible lives. The truth is that many of us have good reason to worry about money. Think about it. Almost everything in our lives comes down to money. Money plays a role in virtually every decision we make, including those that most profoundly affect our lives. Indeed, people often make life-changing decisions based on the presence, abundance, paucity, or absence of money. Marriages and other major relationships may be based wholly or in part on issues of wealth. A 2018 study by TD Ameritrade found that 41 percent of divorced Gen Xers and 29 percent of divorced Boomers report that their marriages ended over money disputes. Failing to come to terms on issues of money is the number one predictor of eventual divorce, according to a 2012 study published in Family Relations, an interdisciplinary journal of applied family science.[1] Depression and sickness are often associated with worry and strife over money.

I'm here to tell you that money shouldn't have control over your life. There's no denying that money is important. If you think of your life as a three-legged stool, health is leg number one, family is leg number two, and money is number three. One, two, and three express

---

1   Catey Hill, "This common behavior is the No. 1 predictor of whether you'll get divorced," *Market-Watch* (January 10, 2018), https://www.marketwatch.com/story/this-common-behavior-is-the-no-1-pre-dictor-of-whether-youll-get-divorced-2018-01-10#:~:text=Data%20released%20Wednesday%20by%20fi-nancial,That%20may%20be%20the%20No.; Jeffrey Dew, Sonya Britt, and Sandra Huston, "Examining the Relationship between Financial Issues and Divorce," *Family Relations: Interdisciplinary Journal of Applied Family Science* (September 4, 2012), https://doi.org/10.1111/j.1741-3729.2012.00715.x

the proper priorities, but the fact is that no stool can stand on fewer than three legs. Take any one leg out, and your life will topple over.

If you don't have money, you cannot enjoy the freedom to live life in the way you choose. Just don't use a shortage of finance as an excuse. Of the three legs, health and family, once lost, cannot readily be replaced. Money? Getting it takes work and attention, that's for sure, but it is the easiest of three legs to fix.

I am living proof that anyone can achieve what they want to achieve if they put their mind to it and their heart back into it. I came from a blue-collar family. Nothing was given to me. I went from working at age thirteen harder than everyone around me, mopping floors and washing dishes, to having the cash to pay for my first car in high school, to teaching myself how to play lacrosse good enough to get me into Division 1, to starting my financial career with a negative net worth due to college debt, to building my business into a multimillion-dollar wealth management firm that serves some of the most successful families in New York.

People often asked me, how did I do this? I will never forget when I first stepped on the lacrosse field at Towson University as a walk-on as a freshman in college. What I recognized, right away, is that everyone was just as good as me, if not better. It was another level, but I had such a desire and passion to play Division One lacrosse that I was ready for the mission.

As each day passed, more and more players were getting cut. Then, all of a sudden, no one else seemed to get cut for a few days. Curious, as the team was finishing their workout in the gym, I approached my head coach, Carl Runk, an amazing coach and person.

"Coach, did I make the team?" I asked.

"Phil, it was really close," he said, "and you are on the fence and most likely not going to make the team. I am sorry, son."

Wow. I was completely crushed. I was used to being the top athlete in high school for many years and never got cut from anything. I walked home feeling so depressed, upset, and lonely. I didn't know anyone from that school and didn't have any family around to comfort me. When I returned to my dorm, the first thing I did was call my mom. I immediately started crying, and of course, like any mom, she tried to comfort me. After speaking to my mom and dad, I went straight to sleep.

The next morning, Coach Kaley, head coach for the Division Two lacrosse team of the New York Institute of Technology (NYIT), called to come home and join his team with a free scholarship. I couldn't believe it. I immediately said yes, but I told him that I was determined to come back to Towson to make this team and play Division One.

He said, "Phil, give us a shot, and after one year, you can do what you want."

I played for NYIT for the spring season and was one of the leading scorers in the division. After that season concluded, I thanked Coach Kaley and said I was going back to Towson.

When I returned to try out for Towson for the second time, I was never so determined in my life to make this team. I was like a horse with blinders on. Nothing was getting in my way of making this team.

Like last time, player after player was getting cut. As we were doing hill repeats with my team, I made it to the top of the hill, breathing quite heavily when Coach Clark, the assistant coach, called my name.

I said, "Yes, Coach Clark?"

He said, "Congratulations, you made the team."

I will never forget that feeling. This was a perfect example that if you really want something, I mean really want something, and you put your mind to it, you will accomplish it!

What did it take? A relentless mind and attitude that always moves me forward and doesn't let me sweat the stupid things in life. In business, I quickly learned how to maximize my own strengths as well as learning how to delegate my weak spots to the expertise of others. If you are burdened by money worries, maybe the universe is telling you to delegate some of the management of your finances to the experts.

So, hear me out. I'm going to give you the keys to success in managing your money.

First and last, it's all about taking control of your money rather than allowing it to control you. Many people know how to make money, but few have any idea of how to manage it effectively. I've seen so many get pulled down by money simply because they allowed their emotions to get the best of them. Yet money can be managed more effectively than just about any other area of your life. From bad investments to bad spending habits, many things can create money trouble. Learn to manage your money—get help managing your money—and you will find that you have taken the first step on the right path, the path to living your best possible life.

Who I Am

I have been managing money for individuals and families for more than twenty years. I started out running my own wealth management group as an employee in several major Wall Street firms before finally jumping out to open my own independent wealth management company. That was the best decision of my career and one of the best in my life. Seeking help managing your money is a positive step, but it is no guarantee that you will get the best advice. Here's why. If you go to Wall Street firms for money management help, you are putting yourself in conflicted hands. If you are going to hire a financial advisor, you want to make sure he or she is a fiduciary on how they manage all aspects of your finances. Many will say, yes, I am a fiduciary, however, they do not share with you that they also have the ability to invest your money outside the fiduciary standard and earn a commission. Having a fiduciary responsibility means they have a duty to put their client's interests before their own. However, a financial advisor in the employ of a big Wall Street firm serves two clients, the firm and you—in that order. There is an inherent conflict of interests here. I know this first hand because I saw it from the inside. I don't like feeling conflicted. In fact, from the get-go, I knew that I wanted to do things differently and that the only way I could was with my own company.

At the start of my career, I was running a fee-based wealth-management practice within a bank. I never had a single client complaint, but I knew in my gut that I was not fully free in the options I could offer. I did my time in these corporate firms for years because I believed I needed a few big brand names on my resume to give me the credibility I needed to build my own business. Allow me a confession.

My belief proved to be unfounded, and today I regret not leaving Wall Street earlier than I did. It wasn't that sticking with the big firms was a waste of time and effort. On the contrary, the experience taught me lessons that have helped me to serve my clients better. But it also taught me what I *didn't* want to do for the rest of my life in finance. And that was a very valuable lesson.

As I built it, Palumbo Wealth Management focuses exclusively on helping clients achieve lives that are "work-optional." This is possible with a good plan. It is possible if you don't make major mistakes. Unfortunately, it's all too easy for us fallible humans to make mistakes. I have seen countless people make tremendous blunders in managing their own money. I, who should know better, have even made similar mistakes with my money in the past. I don't want to live by mistake, and I don't want my clients to live that way. I want to live on purpose, and I want to help my clients live that way, too. So, I'm on a mission to guide my clients to a place in their financial lives where they no longer need to worry about their money. I want to enable them to achieve financial peace of mind *and* start living their lives on their terms.

In this book, I share with you my step-by-step process. It will allow you to create your own path to peace of mind in a work-optional world. You deserve not to worry about money anymore. You only get one life, and managing your money is key to optimizing it. I want you to take on this challenge today, to begin your journey toward work-optional living. I just admitted that I made mistakes in the past. But now, in the present, I am living the work-optional life. You can get there, too. Let's start changing your life.

CHAPTER 1

MONEY: THE OLDEST WORRY IN THE BOOK

My mission is to help people achieve peace of mind about their finances. I'm not talking about "ignorance is bliss." The peace of mind that may result from a lack of awareness or complacency is not serenity but delusion. I want you to be mindful of your money, and I want you to use that mindfulness to give you a legitimate reason not to worry about money or your future.

I've been thinking about this for a long time, at least as far back as my thirteenth year of life. I grew up on Long Island in a blue-collar family. My dad was an electrician, and my mom stayed home to care for my two siblings, Anthony and Rosa, and me. I will never forget the moment I started thinking about money and how dealing with it, managing it, might be my life's work. It was a scorcher of a summer evening. At that time, our home, like many working-class homes, was not air-conditioned. After dinner, my father and I were the only two left sitting at the table. I looked closely at Dad. He didn't notice me looking at him. He had closed his eyes and was shaking his head slowly from side to side, his mouth twisted as if he had just bitten into something unexpectedly bitter.

He exhaled, opened his eyes, and looked toward me.

"What's wrong, Dad?" I asked.

He pushed back from the table, hunched over, placed his elbows on his knees, and shook his head again.

"You know Phil, life really sucks."

Times were hard, and Dad was laid off sometimes three, even six months out of the year. He and Mom had three children to look after. He did not raise his voice, but I took his simple declaration as a warning to me: I could one day be in his shoes.

He really didn't need to say anything for me to know that he was struggling. I could see it in his face and posture. And it hit me hard because he was always amazing, hard-working, and totally dedicated to his family. Even when he was laid off from his regular job, he never gave up. He was always working or hunting down as many side hustles as he could find, just to make ends meet. This was the first time, however, I saw him so discouraged. Maybe it was just the first time I looked hard enough to see it. It hit me in my gut.

He could have given me a lecture or a long complaint. But he did no such thing. He didn't have to. The single sentence and the image he presented to me were supremely eloquent. From that moment, I made my decision. I told myself—in actual words, told myself—to start working as soon as possible so that I would not end up like my dad, a hardworking man with a skill who nevertheless had to worry and struggle until the joy was wrung out of him.

Fortunately, my father instilled a strong work ethic in all of us at home. My siblings and I all worked from a young age. At thirteen, I was already washing dishes and mopping floors at a local restaurant. When most kids were going home from school to hang out with their friends, I played sports right after classes and then headed straight to work until ten or eleven p.m. I hurried home, did my homework, and finally crawled into bed well after midnight. I also worked on Saturdays and Sundays, determined to earn as much extra money as possible. I remember one Sunday morning when my father drove me to the shopping center. I got out of the car. The silence was spooky. And then I realized that I was the only person in the whole place. I leaned up against a wall and waited for my boss to open up. I pictured my friends and their weekend plans, which were devoted to anything but work.

In such moments, I tried not to feel sorry for myself because I was already convinced that I was learning life lessons I would carry with me forever. Besides, my friends' parents were full of praise for my determination. "You should be like Phil," they said. "Look how hard he's working at such a young age!" To this day, that's how they remember me. Their kind words gave me greater confidence in my young life and beyond. I have always appreciated their recognition of my work ethic.

I took pleasure in my work, and I knew I was doing the right thing. But I was also motivated by never wanting to feel the kind of pain my father felt, the worry he had about money. Later, this would guide me toward the field of wealth advisement. It became my job to make sure that the people who came to me would not have to worry about money.

I never wanted to be a doctor, but what I do nevertheless improves both the emotional and physical health of my clients. Stress ages you. And even if you like to work, having to work when you feel more than ready to retire grinds away at you, especially if your occupation is one you no longer care for. I can't tell you how much joy I get out of knowing that what I do for a living helps my clients do all the things they want to do or love to do.

The Traditional Financial World

After more than twenty years as a wealth manager, I've come to understand that, second only to their health and their family's health, the most important thing my clients want to protect is their lifestyle. They want to be able to continue as they are—perhaps with some improvements—and they want to do so while making sure they don't run out of money. The idea that I play a role in helping each of them with such an important aspect of their life is what motivated me to become a wealth manager in the first place. It's a wonderful position to be in, but it also comes with heavy responsibility and self-awareness. My team and I work hard to be the best that we can be. This dedication goes back to my childhood, and it has pushed me to hone my skills in my industry.

As I explained when I introduced myself, I used to run my own team under the umbrella of some of the largest Wall Street wealth management firms. My team and I did excellent work for our clients, but I was serving two masters, the corporation that employed the clients who hired me, and my clients. Corporate executives view their financial advisors as salespeople who must sell the firm's products to keep shareholders happy. There came a point where I did not want to be a fiduciary to the corporation's shareholders. I wanted to serve only my clients. When I finally broke with Wall Street and put my name on my firm, I became the legal fiduciary exclusively of my clients. They know that, under law, my interests come second to theirs—and there is no third-party corporation with shareholders shoving to be served before them.

I do not manufacture any products, and I have no pay-to-play policy arrangement with any investment products. I don't pay a Wall Street firm to sell their products on my platform. My clients never have to worry that I will invest their money to earn a higher commission for myself. My firm's investments are made in the best interest of each client's individual needs. I have no other goal in mind. My clients trust me because I give them every reason to. They see that both of us are focused on the same thing, which is most important to helping each of them realize their own life's vision. Helping people in this way is my own life's vision.

Independent of a larger corporation, I am not limited to the products and services of any single firm. I have access to unlimited resources for my clients. That means I have more freedom to help you reach a very powerful point in your life, the point at which work becomes optional. You can take work or leave it or take some of it and leave the rest. You can work when you want to or when you need to, and you can do so with perfect peace of mind. That is what I did when I left Wall Street to start Palumbo Wealth Management. I knew what kind of lifestyle I wanted, and I also knew that the work-optional concept was something I wanted for myself. I had worked long enough as a wealth manager to understand that I *could* take charge of my own financial and vocational destiny. If I could shape my own destiny, I could help others refashion theirs.

Traditional Retirement

I had walked away from the traditional financial world. I realized that I was now perfectly positioned to help my clients walk away from the traditional concept of retirement.

The very word "retirement" is crammed full of emotion. Traditionally, retirement is viewed as arriving at a certain age, which usually coincides with someone's Social Security benefits or pension eligibility and aligns with what the potential retiree's friends or relatives have chosen for themselves. My grandfather, for instance, spent his working life doing arduous labor as a boiler worker for Con Ed, New York's power utility. When I was in my early twenties, he told me a story I will never forget. One day, he was working on a scaffold in the boiler room when a coworker and close friend fell from it and was killed instantly. At that moment, my sixty-two-year-old grandfather decided to retire. It was a decision triggered by intense emotion, but it was also a reasonable decision. Along with Social Security, Granddad had a good pension and some Con Ed stock, which paid dividends. As he was not a big spender, he could comfortably afford a traditional retirement, in which he simply stopped working.

For my grandfather, his Con Ed stock and Social Security were important, of course, but his pension was the cornerstone. Today, the pension, which used to be a common feature of a good long-term job, is a vanishing benefit. In its place are 401k plans, which offer valuable income tax deferments and, depending on the extent of the employer's matching contribution, can be very helpful. But the fact remains that, today, the burden of saving for retirement is pretty much wholly on the shoulders of the employee. Even if your employer matches your contributions generously, the 401k is not a replacement for the old-time pension, which, in many cases, could see a person all the way through retirement. In fact, prior to the 1980s, most retirees were wholly dependent on their pension, which was built by an employer, who made certain estimates about their workforce and how long, on average, a retired employee would live. Based on these actuarial assumptions, the employer put aside money, and, come retirement, the former worker could rely on the combination of pension and Social Security to live out the rest of his or her life, barring mishap or carelessness, in reasonable comfort.

The problem with pensions? Well, they were basically doomed. People started living longer even as inflation became a virtually permanent fixture of American life. Pensions became increasingly more difficult and costly to administer. Many companies began to find that their pensions were chronically underfunded. Their solution was to offer their employees "defined contribution plans." And as that name implies, the employee defines the contribution amount and how that money is invested. After the 1980s, these defined contribution plans, including 401k plans, became increasingly common, and fewer and fewer traditional pension plans remain active today.

Pension plans are also known as "defined benefit plans" because the employer defines an income benefit for the employee at a certain age until death. In defined contribution plans, including 401k's, the employee uses pre-tax income to make contributions (a Roth 401k is a special case, which uses after-tax income), which may be matched by the employer. What is important to recognize is that the risk is transferred from employers to employees with the goal that when they retire, they will have enough money amassed in their 401k to help them live comfortably.

According to the Investment Company Institute, as of September 2020, Americans have saved up $33.1 trillion dollars for retirement. Out of that amount, $6.5 trillion is held in 401k plans. Is the combination of 401k savings and non-401k savings a sufficient substitute for the combination of savings and a traditional pension? That depends on what the employee has contributed and what the employer's matching contribution has been.

Of course, there is the important addition of Social Security. But even this is increasingly subject to doubt. The worrisome question is: *Can individuals and families rely on Social Security even being there for them when they fully retire?* According to the Social Security Administration, Social Security Trust Fund reserves are projected to be tapped out by 2037. This means that many retirees in the near future may not be able to rely on receiving income from Social Security, despite having paid into the system, by law, through FICA payroll taxes. The Social Security Administration says that Social Security benefits are intended to replace about 37 percent of past earnings for a person who has worked all their adult life for an "average" wage and retires at sixty-five. This is a significant replacement portion of an "average" income, so it is no wonder that Social Security benefits are an important and common income stream in retirement. The thought of no longer having it is ample reason for concern.

Whether you are contemplating traditional retirement or a work-optional status, which may include some continuation of earned income, it is important to know where your portfolio of income streams will come from after you leave the full-time "obligatory" workforce. Will this array support the lifestyle you currently have? Will you have to cut back? Or can you structure a scenario in which your lifestyle is actually enhanced?

Most often, in addition to Social Security, income streams come from personal savings, investment accounts, retirement accounts (such as 401k's), and real estate. For business owners who have withdrawn from active involvement in the firm, there are many cases in which an owner continues to enjoy income from the business while it is functioning under the leadership of another family member. Alternatively, an owner may choose to sell her business. Either way, the extra assets can generate important income streams if handled correctly.

Walking Away from Work

So, we come to the big question. How much income do you need after leaving the traditional workforce?

The big answer? It depends …

The most productive first step you can take is to change your thinking about work and retirement and focus instead on what is possible for you to achieve. The traditional thinking was—and for many still is—dead simple: *I want to retire on this day, and this is how much I need.*

Why reduce yourself to a dead simple number? Why not consider taking the opportunity to rewrite a tired old script?

Think about reaching a point in your life when you can walk away from work, rendering it strictly optional. This is committing neither to retirement nor to continuing to grind away at a job you may or may not enjoy, let alone love. To be able to live a work-optional life, you need to have saved diligently and invested productively. You need to make a plan that lists all the steps you must take to position yourself for such a life. This book guides you through those steps. But understand that the universal reality of economics is scarcity. This means that not everyone can have everything they want. No wonder the nineteenth-century English writer-philosopher Thomas Carlyle dubbed economics the "dismal science"! Out of all the assets we each need, the scarcest of all is time. So, it is not surprising that the problem I most frequently encounter with my clients is that they have waited too long to plan, save, and invest.

It may surprise you to learn that most people don't know what they want out of life, and if they have set some goal or goals for themselves, they don't know if it's possible to attain them. Even those relatively few who have an inkling of the concept of making work optional have no idea how to get to that point or even how to measure progress toward it. When I first talk to this majority about the state of their finances, most tell me they have their finances "in their heads." A few tell me that they have gotten so far as to pound out a to-do list of financial ideas and inspirations. The list is sitting in their iPhone Notes app. When the notions are in their heads or on their phones, they never become actualized. Most people never take the next step forward, yet fewer take a step back to survey a much larger vision for their lives. If you step neither forward nor back, you can never get a handle on what you need to do to live at the level you want from day to day or month to month. It's as basic as this: Most folks have no clear understanding of how much they need to save and therefore how much they can spend to reach their goals—provided they have even set those goals.

I am not talking about poor people, uneducated people, or naïve people. Consider this. One of my clients, a senior executive at a Fortune 500 company, traveled the world for his company. One day, while they were in Miami for a company event, his wife became very ill very fast. She had a piercing headache, which turned out to be the symptom of an embolism. Fortunately, she received prompt treatment and survived. But the experience was eye-opening for both my client and his wife. He was just fifty-five at the time and had not even begun to think about walking away from work. But now he knew exactly what he wanted to do.

"Phil, I really want to stop working."

His wife's health situation loomed as a big wake-up call for him, and he now wanted to change his life. Before her near-death experience, he thought nothing of getting on a jet to travel halfway around the world for facetime with high-level executives. This did not leave a lot of time to be his wife. He was so engaged in his own work life that he didn't realize that he was no longer fully living. The headache that nearly killed the woman he loved drove him to make big changes.

"Phil, am I at the point where work is optional for me? Can I walk away from work today and never look back? Can I dedicate my days to my family instead of to my job?"

I couldn't tell him, not off the top of my head. He had a basic financial plan in place, but he and I needed to take a deep-dive analysis to evaluate all the options. We needed to acquire a greater understanding of his total assets and his annual spending. I understood his sense of urgency, but I knew better than to let his urgency push me to take potentially harmful shortcuts. Together, methodically, we developed a full analysis of what exactly would occur if he stopped working today. Could he walk away from it all and start to spend more time with his wife? What would it cost him to start living his life with her instead of being tied down to a position that allowed no time for anything else?

In the end, the results of a thorough analysis brought him tremendous relief. He had always been a diligent saver. He had not taken on a lot of debt to fund a lavish lifestyle. For him, work was now truly optional, and we had the numbers to prove it.

My client had two advantages in getting to this point. First, he had a demanding but well-paying leadership position. Second, while we had never before put together a plan for him to leave work at fifty-five—the thought had never before entered his head—we had planned together for him to eventually get to this point. The planning paid off. He didn't have a lot of debt. His mortgage was paid off. He was a great saver. Through the years, we mapped out his finances, investing strategically and conservatively. He had built financial freedom. Only through a careful analysis that looked at all the available options did it become apparent that he could leave regular employment right now—and not only leave it but pursue whatever he wanted to pursue.

With data-based knowledge and analytical insight, my client recognized that he was free. With freedom came the realization that he didn't want to retire entirely. He wanted to walk away from his job but not from work, optional as it now was. He ended up staying at home for some time while picking up work locally here and there, earning a side income that came without any of the time-sucking stress of his full-time job. He could work and remain relevant in his industry, but he now had ample time for his wife and family. They started living in a way, he now realized, that he had long desired.

Because of financial planning, my client was able to stop fixating on traditional retirement and change his goal to achieving a work-optional lifestyle. You have one life. You don't want to say to yourself: *Well, at age sixty-two, sixty-five, or seventy, when I'm eligible for Social Security benefits, I'll maybe be able to retire.* Why relinquish that control? You should be able to ask yourself: *At what point in* my *life can work become optional? When will I no longer need to worry about my money?* If you plan, save, and invest properly now, you will be able to take on life, including later life, with confidence, on your terms, and even walk away from work, or at least work as traditionally conceived if you decide that is what you want.

Today, we are living in a much different world than that of thirty or forty years ago. Technology has transformed businesses. In varying degrees, practically everything is digital. Many people have the option of working from home and perhaps spending more time with their families. I see that in my practice, as many of my clients can now work part-time consulting in their areas of special expertise and make very good money, all in the comfort of their homes. This is a game-changer. It used to be that when you retired on a pension and Social Security, there weren't many work-from-home opportunities. Our world runs differently now. People are living longer and often healthier, their capacity to make money and contribute materially to society undiminished.

If that is what they want *to do!*

I'm not saying that the ability and option to work beyond the traditional retirement years is universally preferable, let alone mandatory. Traditional retirement or even early retirement is a fine goal—if you have the financial means and if that is what you want. But anything that gives you greater control and more options is an absolute good. It is possible to prepare in the present to develop more control over your future. You can take back the power over your own career and your own life. The options are abundant.

The Three Stages of Making Work Optional

Most of you will decide to retire between the ages of sixty and sixty-five. That's neither a good nor a bad strategy. It is simply a fact. It is the default plan, and it may be the right plan for *you*. But it is also a fact that, thanks to the economic, scientific, political, and technological progress of today's civilization, we have moved well beyond the average human life expectancy that prevailed in 1940 when Social Security went into effect in the United States: just sixty-three years. In essence, Social Security promised a reward to those who beat the odds by living past sixty-five. Today, we can expect to live years beyond sixty-five—twenty, thirty, even nearly forty. These added years belong to us. I want my clients to be able to use them not just comfortably but optimally and on their own terms.

Let's look more closely at the numbers. By the age of sixty to sixty-five, males have a 50 percent chance of living to eighty-six. The statistics for women at sixty to sixty-five are even better. They have a 50 percent chance of reaching eighty-eight. For married couples, statistics tell us that at least one spouse will live to ninety-two. Now, dig into these numbers. It is likely that you will pass through three stages of health and wellness as you grow older. From about sixty to eighty, the first period, you will probably enjoy the most energy and wellness and will still be able to travel and engage in such leisure activities as golf, swimming, hiking, biking—whatever you like. Most people between eighty and eighty-five tend to slow down. We call this second stage the middle years, a period when things start to become calmer and quieter. You're not engaging in as many activities, and you're probably not spending as much money. After eighty-five, there is usually a marked winding down. During these years, health issues may arise and impose limitations. It is a mistake to think only as far as, say, sixty-five. There are years to come, and these years bring their own changes. "Retirement"—whatever form that takes for you—is a continuation of living, and the three stages of life after retirement are something to think about and plan for as you map your future.

Whatever the Goal, it's Possible

The idea behind my *work optional* concept is not to wait until you're sixty-five to officially call it quits on mandatory work. Instead, plan and act in ways that give you the confidence to say *yes* when you arrive at your retirement target year—*Yes! Work is now optional!*

Sixty-five does not have to be the default age for this declaration. Maybe for you, the age is fifty or fifty-five. Maybe it is later. Either way, the earlier you make a plan, the more options you have for creating the security you need and the peace of mind you want. You won't be locked in. If at some point you want to walk away from work or if working part-time is appealing, you'll likely have created a financial situation that enables whatever choice you make. The great thing about it is that the earlier you're able to achieve this for yourself, the longer you'll have to enjoy your most active years.

During this time, your mind is sharper, your body is able, and you can pursue more of the things that you love.

I advise each of my clients to take a step back and ask themselves: *What is my vision for the rest of my life?* Ask this, and you can dig deeper into the financial requirements of that vision. You can arrive at *your* number. What do you need on an after-tax basis to live your vision? Once you define and understand what you want for your life, you must ask yourself if you have or will have sufficient savings and/or passive income streams to maintain your desired lifestyle through your remaining years. From where are your different income streams going to come? As we've mentioned, these streams may include any or all of these: a pension, Social Security, real estate income, or business income. Maybe you plan to continue working part-time or freelance—perhaps in your current field or industry or in something different. Whatever your situation, the most important part of figuring out your income streams is understanding your vision and its associated costs. Armed with that number, you can determine the mix of income streams that will enable you to realize your vision.

The key to reaching your financial goals and making work optional is cultivating a strong, positive mindset that will drive you through the three steps I have outlined. Step one is creating a vision for what you want the rest of your life to look like. Step two is understanding what the cost of attaining that vision will be. Step three is asking yourself how you can arrive at the realization of that vision as fast as possible. Thinking is required. Don't focus on the default retirement ages that mark Social Security eligibility. For that matter, don't fixate on any other arbitrary target. Think instead about when *you* want to arrive at a point where work becomes optional. Then shape your mindset to get you to that point as quickly as you can. Don't settle for somehow automatically aging into it.

This proactive approach to what is, after all, your own and one and only life starts with and depends on building a viable financial plan, which will tell you when that work-optional day will come. Once you get there and have full confidence that work has in fact become optional, you will have the freedom to act.

Let me put what I have just said into context. Finance—money—is necessary to living a fully satisfying life in which work is optional. But, while necessary, money is not sufficient. Think of a satisfying life as a three-legged stool. Finance is leg number three, and family is number two. Health is leg number one. As Confucius put it thousands of years ago, "We all have two lives, until we realize we have one. When we are healthy we want 10,000 things, and when we are sick, we want one thing." Getting your money right with a sound financial plan will contribute to good health by enabling you to get the best medical advice and treatment available and, maybe even more importantly, by reducing energy-sapping stress. But money cannot guarantee your good health.

Health, in turn, will enable you to enjoy your family, the second leg supporting your stool. But enjoying your family becomes difficult if you are continually burdened by worry about money.

A three-legged stool requires the presence of all three legs, and the leg over which you have the most direct and effective control is your money. The earlier you create a plan for managing money, the greater the likelihood that you will live the rest of your life in financial freedom. Money management is not rocket science, but we can learn this much from rocket scientists: While it is possible to course-correct after launching a rocket, the earlier you determine the optimum trajectory, the greater your odds of reaching your target. In financial planning, the earlier you invest time and effort in building a plan so that you understand your future trajectory, the more options you have for actually creating the trajectory that will reach your target.

For those of you reading this book who are in your forties, fifties, or sixties, you still have options. That's the good news. But I have even better. You may already be in a position where work is optional and not even realize it. So, read on, and find out exactly how to achieve the biggest, most consequential goals you have set for your life. I will take you through the planning process step by step.

CHAPTER 2

CHANGING WHAT RETIREMENT MEANS

Picture this: You've planned everything very well. Now you're in the driver's seat. You get to call all the shots. Maybe you decide to walk away earlier than expected. Why? Because you can. You are now free to find part-time work that you enjoy or to take up a new hobby or a volunteer program that is meaningful to you. Maybe you want to start a new company or dive into a project that's always been on the back burner.

This is how *work optional* can fit into your overall plan. The bottom line is that you now have the option to do whatever you like. In the financial service industry, retirement is an overused and obsolete term. The word itself should be retired and replaced with "work-optional." Imagine that you have saved enough money and invested wisely with your work-optional strategy; maybe you own real estate that generates income or have a business that can create passive assets. Now you've reached the point where you have sufficient resources to live at the same economic level you enjoyed at the height of your conventional work earnings. The difference is that your lifestyle is in fact better than ever because you are not obliged to work.

Work-optional works for you because you work only when and if you want to, not because you must. Most people right now are in the "working because I have to" phase of life. Work-optional is available to those who have purposefully chosen to continue working, even though they've already achieved a financially feasible retirement. They no longer need to work to sustain their lives. They've put a good plan into action and have designed a lifestyle that ensures financial peace of mind. They are free to work for the sheer joy of it.

What defines "work-optional"?

- You're doing only the things that you love.
- You're doing these things only when and where you want to do them.
- You're doing these things only for the people for whom you want to do them.
- You're not in need of the money. It's a bonus that comes with the pleasure and satisfaction of doing work that is meaningful to you.

The key decision you need to make is whether you want to completely stop working entirely or work part-time at something you enjoy. If you're thinking about stopping, you must ask yourself at least two basic but difficult questions:

What will I do day-to-day and hour after hour?
How will I find fulfillment in each day for the rest of my life?

If you're a golfer, how many days a week can you golf and still enjoy going out to the course? If you enjoy dining in interesting restaurants, how many times can you do that per week without getting bored? If you love watching Netflix, how many hours a day will you sit on the couch and stream shows? If you don't have a hobby, what will you do to occupy your days? If you want to vacation, how many trips are you comfortable taking each year? It's important to think through the details and figure out what feels right for you. One thing I will say based on my experience working exclusively with families and individuals who are preparing to retire is they are all happy they did it and really enjoy this chapter very much.

Why Are People Working Later in Life?

Traditionally, entering retirement signaled a need to pull in your horns and watch your pennies. People didn't just retire from their job. They at least partially retired from life, purposely spending less than they spent when they had a regular paycheck. Many of today's retirees live their retirement far differently from how my grandfather lived his. The biggest difference is that many spend money equal to what they had spent while working. In fact, some spend more because they now have time for more non-free leisure activities, such as vacationing, buying a second home, dining out, and shopping. The lifestyles of the retiree are moving closer to the lifestyles of the rich and famous.

And there is nothing wrong with that—if you have set yourself up for it by planning early and wisely.

We should also note here that the decision to fully retire is often determined by the type of career you had when fully engaged in the workforce. Both my grandfather and father were blue-collar guys who worked physically demanding jobs. Granddad worked on huge ConEd boilers, and Dad was an electrician, who commuted into Manhattan every working day, climbed ladders, snaked through crawl spaces, and sweated for every dollar he earned. Over time, intensive, physical labor wears on your body. For blue-collar guys and gals, retirement is often seen as a well-earned rest for weary bones. For my father, retirement was an easy decision. He was ready to step out of the daily grind and claim his well-earned rest. Besides, in his day, steady part-time work was not easy to come by. The gig economy did not yet exist as an alternative to "regular" employment.

Today, much of the blue-collar has given way to the white-collar. Most jobs no longer make heavy physical demands. Among my own clients, for example, many are professionals—lawyers, physicians, executives, accountants, and the like. Their bodies don't cry out for restful retirement. At sixty or older, they are still both physically and mentally capable of doing the kind of work they did when they were fully employed. Some are self-employed business owners, physicians, and professional advisors who work on a part-time basis and exercise control over their time, deciding on their own hours and availability. Often, working remotely from home is a perfectly viable option. The relative ease in remote work pace and lifestyle makes continuing work, part-time, an increasingly attractive option. Not only is work-optional employment not detrimental to health and wellbeing, but it also promotes these good things.

When it does feel like time to step away from full-time employment, making the retirement decision often comes down to the type of career you had and the degree of love and passion you still have for it. For most people today, managing retirement is no longer a binary decision. You don't have to remain in a regular job or step away from the world of work. You can work part-time, even if doing so requires some retooling and reinvention of yourself. If you cannot do part-time work in your field, perhaps you can become a consultant in that field? Or you may want to seize the opportunity to get involved in an industry that you had always wanted to explore but never had the time to do it. Are you interested in starting a small business? Perhaps you frequently talked about doing so but never before had the time or the courage to act on it.

Working part-time at something you love may well let you step away from the daily grind without irrevocably leaving behind the world of work. In addition to creating an income stream and productively occupying your mind and imagination, part-time employment often keeps you socialized. This, together with an active mind applied to a productive enterprise, gives you a sense of self-worth and relevance in the world. You'll still have time for the leisure stuff, but engagement and involvement in work are good for body and soul.

Best of all, you are not locked in. Visitors and newcomers to our shores are often amazed by the degree to which Americans identify themselves with their work. When an American meets someone new, you can bet that one of the very first questions asked is, "What do you do?" Work-optional gives you the opportunity to break out of the constraints of your old identity and try something new if you like.

Provided that you have saved up enough money and/or have other robust income sources, you are free to start something new and to do so with limited risk. This is a function of true freedom, and it is the place to which I want to take you, guided, of course, by your own plans and pathway.

Working well into your later years can pay off in more than money. For many, it is indispensable to their emotional and physical health, but you never want to have to punch a clock when you're into or past traditional retirement age. You should be living on your own terms and on your own schedule and according to when and how you want to work. Yes, a recent Harvard Medical School study lists many valid reasons why people are working later in life. We all live longer, most jobs require less brute-force physical work, people in their sixties today are in better health today than this age cohort was fifty years ago and working can feel good and improve your health. Some studies have linked working past retirement with better health and longevity.

All this is terrific, and all of it true, but we cannot ignore the dark side. If work past retirement is a grim necessity rather than a happy choice, it can be detrimental instead of beneficial to your health. Suffering stress on the job has long been recognized as a risk factor for coronary artery disease and stroke, conditions to which older people are vulnerable. While jobs tend to be less physical these days, older workers who take on more physically demanding work are at increased risk of injury. Finally, for all too many people, retirement is not greeted as a welcome reward for a life of labor. If you feel your job lacks meaning, if you're bored by it, or if you feel burned out, stress and depression loom as real dangers—especially if you are an older worker. It is therefore critically important to create freedom for yourself by arranging your life to make work optional.

Ridding Yourself of Archaic Thinking

During the Covid-19 pandemic, I noticed that many people who had been contemplating retirement finally decided to draw a line in the sand and stop working completely. One of my longtime clients falls into this very category. One day, he called me: "Phil, this pandemic has really been taxing on me. I'm thinking about selling my dental practice. Do you feel like I'm at a point in my life where work is optional for me?"

After we hung up, I gathered all the necessary information I needed to perform a thorough analysis to assist my client in understanding his options. I quickly saw that if he sold his business for a certain amount of money, he would be at a place where work was optional for him. He and his wife met me for dinner that night, and I took out my iPad to show him the numerical data. I quickly proved to them that after all their hard work saving, creating a plan with me, and continuing down the path toward financial freedom, they were now ready to take the leap. For all their years of diligence, they were now at a place where they could easily sell the business and move on with their lives.

After selling his business, my client decided that he'd love to continue doing some consulting work within the dental industry. That way, he could still make a good amount of income to supplement his other resources. This desire was a choice, not a grim necessity. As I said, I created a plan for him and his wife years earlier, and I was able to prove to them that they had made it! They attained the point where work had become optional for them.

I love delivering such news to my clients because every single time I can see the excitement in their faces. Now, this partially retired dentist and his wife can go anywhere in the world. He can still do consulting work within his field. He's not strapped to a business and a daily nine-to-five job requiring his physical presence every single moment. He can still have some income coming in while also doing all the other things he and his wife enjoy.

This is the payoff of shifting a retirement mindset to a work-optional mindset. Make this shift, and you are on the road to a place at which work becomes optional. This gives you a measure of freedom that most of us strive for. You liberate yourself instead of waiting for the little hand on the clock to reach the arbitrary hour that marks "official" retirement. Shift your mindset, and you may discover that work optional begins at age fifty, fifty-two, or maybe fifty-five—years before you anticipated it would and regardless of what the clock tells you. Now, my dentist was fortunate that he still liked dentistry—certainly liked it enough to want to keep his hand in as a consultant. Knowing that you have the option of planning an earlier work-optional exit is even more urgently important for the many people out there in the world today who have discovered that they do not enjoy the career path they have chosen. Such a person, discovering that the work-optional moment is arriving sooner than the hour of "official" retirement, can rejoice in the option of starting over in a new career, perhaps in a field or industry that excites them. The options are limited only by the individual's imagination, and the newfound freedom is exhilarating.

Life Expectancy Chart

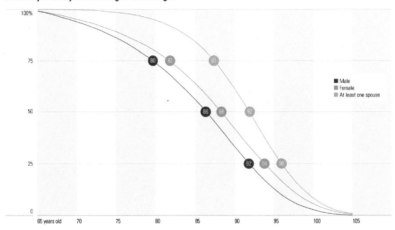

Retirees Should Plan for a Long Retirement
Probability of a 65-year-old Living to Various Ages

Source: 2012 Individual Annuity Mortality Basic Tables, Society of Actuaries. © Morningstar 2022 and Precision Information, dba Financial Fitness Group 2022. All Rights Reserved.

CHAPTER 3

INSTIGATE A PLAN, CREATE A COURSE OF ACTION

*T*o *instigate* is a synonym for *to initiate*, but it has the connotation of *to incite.* I like that connotation because it conveys the idea that you need to *incite* yourself to shift your mindset from traditional retirement to a state of being in which work is optional. Perhaps you have a vague sense that things could be better for you, but because things seem to be working out well enough, you don't feel any urgency about going through the trouble of making a plan to change, let alone transform, your status quo. *If it ain't broke ...* well, you know the rest.

Look, I never force my clients to do anything, and I'm not about to force you. But I do hope I can *incite* you to *instigate* a plan that will give you control over your financial future and that will stake a claim on greater freedom to choose among multiple options, including the option to make work itself optional.

Make no mistake, creating a plan—charting a course of action—is essential to achieving a work-optional status. The financial mechanics necessary to implement this concept must be in place to ensure that you are spending less than you earn and investing the difference until that investment amount is capable of generating enough surplus income *now* to support you for the rest of your life *later.* If you start early, time is on your side. Money, like a living organism, takes time to grow. But the longer you wait to instigate your plan, the more the alliance between you and time will erode. Ultimately, it disintegrates completely. Time will become your enemy in a battle for your freedom—freedom from worry about money and freedom to say goodbye to your "normal" (status quo) work schedule, so that you can work or not work on your own terms. I can't tell you that having a plan now will extend your lifetime. I can promise you that adding freedom to whatever time you have will elevate the value of that time beyond measure.

With my clients, no matter their annual spending ability, we are always able to build a plan that provides a realistic financial scope for achieving realistic life goals—provided the plan is instigated early enough, monitored, adjusted as need be, and followed. I'm hoping that, if you've picked up this book, you probably don't need another jab-in-the-ribs reminder of the blessings and freedom of work optional.

At the risk of repeating myself, I want to remind you that the old mindset of retirement as total withdrawal from the world of work is no longer a universal goal. It is the product of a bygone world that was modeled on the tube sock—that is, *One Size Fits All.* Isn't it better to find or create the one size that fits *you*—perfectly?

Tube-sock-era retirement requires that you walk away from work and live on whatever savings or income streams you have, adjusting your lifestyle—downward, if necessary—to ensure that you don't outlive your financial resources. Abandoning the one-size-fits-all mindset to embrace the quest for the one size that fits *you* requires that you make and execute a financial plan to position you so that work will become optional because you have sufficient reserves and income streams to maintain your desired standard of living without the need for employment. You are not retired. You are work-optional.

Instigating a work-optional financial plan begins by asking yourself what your new vision is for your life—now and in the future. If that vision includes maintaining your current lifestyle while making work optional, you know that the financial plan you create cannot not rely on your earning one penny more than you do now.

Getting a new client to think outside the status quo typically takes some patient prodding. I often ask prospective clients to tell me what they're looking to accomplish in their life. Most respond with a blank stare—at least at first. I leave that question hanging in the air and then ask them to enumerate the sources from which they intend to accumulate income. Investments, such as stocks and bonds? Dividend investments? Real estate investments? Rental properties? Other sources of "passive income," which are earnings from sources other than an employer or contractor—in other words, work.

Finally, I ask them if they have a financial plan. Sometimes, I get that blank stare again. Some prospective clients tell me that their current advisor's plan is not working well. Others just respond with a simple no. Most often, though, what I hear is *Yes, but it's just in my head. I know what I need to do.* A financial plan is a contract with yourself, and like any other unwritten contract, it's not worth the paper it's written on. You need a well-reasoned and realistic plan, thought out, plotted out, and set down.

What Does it Take to Make a Plan?

The first requirement is a willingness to take stock of your situation, your reality, your needs, our desires, your aspirations, and your fears. Having taken full and honest stock of these things, you need to commit to creating a plan with the understanding that a plan is, first and last, a course of action. It is not an abstract analysis, it is not a wish list, and it is not a theory. It is more akin to an assembly manual, a set of instructions to guide *actions* that will build something you want: a new shed, an outdoor barbecue, a playground set, whatever. Like any plan, an assembly manual is without value until it is put into action.

Now, if you aren't comfortable with a screwdriver and wrench, even the best set of assembly instructions is unlikely to be translated into action with a high degree of success. I tell each of my clients that the probability of their successfully executing the financial plan we create together requires that it be put into action in the proper way. Failing to do this makes the odds of a successful outcome pretty slim. Of course, you can go through your life without a financial plan. Many people have done it, and many more people will do it. Drawing up a written financial plan—a contract with yourself—will, however, put you steps ahead. Creating and expressing a thoughtful, reality-based vision for your life gives you clarity and understanding. Having a plan takes work, but the plan makes it much easier for you to understand, evaluate, go after, and reach your goals. Moreover, the plan itself reduces worry because you can see each step that needs to be taken. Sooner or later, people with a plan for "retirement" worry that they have not saved enough or invested effectively enough to maintain their quality of life in their later years. In fact, they may spend much of the time they have leading up to those later years worrying rather than taking action. Making a plan takes work. Thinking is required. But, in the long run, the plan makes everything easier.

I have dedicated my working life to building financial plans for my clients, and I am *not* suggesting that you must spend even an hour or two every day writing in a journal or mapping out all the small details. But I do recommend that you determine your main or overarching goal and then write out, to the extent that you can, your long-term vision for your life.

Why do this?

So that you know everything you want to achieve. Unless you can set this down in words, you are aiming at a target that does not exist. The good news is that this "assignment" sounds more daunting than it is. Simply take the time to sit back, relax, and ask yourself: *What is it that I'm looking to accomplish in my life? How do I see my future?* And then add a third question: *Why am I doing what I do now?*

Once you have clearly answered these questions, you yourself will be able to understand the details of what comes next: your financial need and what it is going to take to satisfy this need so that you can transform your vision for your life into reality. Building out a written financial plan based on these answers helps to optimize your wealth and realize your dreams.

I will never forget a meeting with one prospective client. Our chat that day began by talking through all his numbers. He came to the meeting armed with all the specifics: *I have a home that's worth two million dollars, I own an investment property worth three million dollars, I have a retirement account worth one million dollars, and this is my Social Security income ....*

He knew his numbers, but I could see from his unyielding grimace that he felt a high level of anxiety even as he reeled off his numbers. I stopped him mid-sentence.

"Relax. Sit back and take a breath. We'll get to the rest of your numbers, but, right now, talk to me about how you see the rest of your life. What's your vision for that? How do you want to live? How do you see yourself in the next five, ten, fifteen years? In other words, what do you want?"

If I hadn't seen it happen many, many times before, I wouldn't have believed it. His grimace fell away, he smiled—for the first time since he had walked into my office—and the conversation became laid back, as he calmly discussed what he wanted in the coming years.

I'm not a magician, a psychiatrist, or a hypnotist. When he walked in, he assumed I didn't care much about what *he* wanted for *his* life. He believed—mistakenly—that all I wanted was a report of his numbers and nothing more. He found that call to account for himself highly stressful. I do need to dig into the numbers, of course, but my goal is to help people to live their lives in the very best ways that they possibly can. I need to know the person *before* I get to the numbers. A lot of people think that getting down to business with a financial advisor means a narrow focus on data. What good are numbers if you bury the person in them?

To me, the most important dialogue between client and wealth manager is the one that helps the wealth manager better understand the client on a personal level—and, for that matter, helps the client better understand himself. It cannot be just facts and calculators and elevated chatter about money. First and last, it needs to be a personalized conversation aimed at discovering where the client wants to be and helping him get there.

When I asked him to tell me about his vision for his life, he started telling me about his grandchildren, his hobbies, about his desire to start a small business, perhaps. He talked about how he'd always dreamed of traveling with his wife and wanted to see the world. He had already relaxed as he laid out his vision, and I took great pleasure in telling him that all these things were within reach.

For me, the greatest thing about that meeting was that when he began to share with me his visions and dreams for the rest of his life, his pained face brightened into a smile. I apologize for the cliché, but it really was what you feel when you see the clouds part on a gloomy day and the sun break through. All I had done was invite him to participate in an exercise that he had never considered before: talk about what *he* wanted! Knee-deep in the rat race, grinding away every day, never taking a step back to reflect, it never occurred to him to ask himself what he really wanted.

What is it that I'm working so hard for?

What do I want my life to look and feel like?

I have these meetings all the time, and each time they are eye-opening for me, yes, but even more for my clients. All I do is ask and invite. *They* give themselves incredible perspective on how to prioritize what's important. The numbers are necessary. But the meeting is not all about the numbers.

I tell people that creating a work-optional plan is like running a marathon. Think about the prospect of running twenty-six-plus miles. There's incredible preparation and planning that goes into getting across that finish line. You need to think about every mile, strategizing the distribution of your energy and effort so that you do not peak too early or too late but deliver the most efficient and effective performance for the long haul. Planning a marathon is very different from planning a sprint. Yet what I find frustrating is that so many people devote so much time to the sprints in their lives and so little to life itself. They spend more time working through details of a vacation or which car they're going to purchase than to create a vision for their future. It takes energy, diligence, and strategic thinking to plot out the course of your life, especially when what you want is to make work optional.

LAYING OUT THE REST OF YOUR LIFE

Over twenty years of helping individuals and families plan their financial future, I have come to recognize that most people who do not plan their finances effectively or at all are fearful of what they might discover. Many people believe they will never be able to retire, much less walk away from working whenever they feel like it. They don't examine their situation much less make a plan because they don't want confirmation of their fears. As for making work optional, the idea is so foreign and seems so remote that they don't even bother to look into it.

Most people who believe that they will never have enough money saved to support their fully employed lifestyle make no serious attempt to confirm or refute their belief. Depending on when these doubts come in life—early or late—the doubters may be right to doubt. It may be too late to accumulate enough money to walk away from work. It may be too late to go into retirement living the same lifestyle you had when you were fully employed. But why give up? You can never do anything great in life if you do not learn and face the facts straight on. The issues we are dealing with are not necessarily binary matters of either/or. If you have not planned early enough or effectively enough, you may not be able to live work-optional. But it is likely that you still have time to improve your financial life and manage your savings and income streams as well as they possibly can be managed. Never let the best become the enemy of the good. Refusing to make yourself knowledgeable only takes you farther off course and farther from your goals. Seek an advisor. When you learn what is possible and what is not, you will have an easier time managing your expectations and, if necessary, modifying your goals. The less you know, the fewer options you have.

CHAPTER 4

YOU KNOW WHAT YOU WANT: THIS IS HOW YOU START

The key to reaching a point where work becomes optional is understanding how much your desired lifestyle will cost per year. This is not about you putting together a constraining budget or retreating from the level of your fully employed lifestyle by introducing new limits to your quality of life. Whether or not you consider yourself wealthy, know this: wealthy people do not like the idea of living within a budget. Instead, they have a smarter and bolder take on spending. They plan to invest whatever money they possibly can. Whatever is left over is what can be spent. It is discretionary money.

At first glance, this may look shamelessly indulgent. But just think about it. This attitude puts the priority emphasis on *investment* (outlays that generate income) while *spending* (outlays that create loss) is reserved for the remainder only. No wonder this approach has produced so much wealth. And it is just such wealth that puts a person in a work-optional position sooner rather than later.

Now, work-optional is one form or expression of "financial freedom." But one size does not fit all. You must ask yourself: *What constitutes financial freedom* for me? It's different for everyone, but it's certainly achievable if you chart the course, in a timely manner, and take the right steps beginning immediately.

Realize the Vision: Start Now

Two steps toward accumulating wealth are essential.

Step 1: Save your money.

Step 2: Invest in asset classes that have performed well over time. How much money you earn matters less than how much money you save. I have met many people who make one or two million a year or even more and spend every penny. Even these high-earning non-savers are not going to attain anything like a work-optional goal.

I will never forget a prospective client who visited me at my office after hearing a lecture I hosted. He had a $2.5 million portfolio he wanted me to review. When I asked him how much annual income he averaged throughout his career, he answered $35,000. I almost fell off my chair. I could not even imagine someone amassing such a large portfolio after earning on average $35,000 per year. Then he told me his story.

This man, it turned out, was *the* poster child for the importance of saving and investing early on. From the get-go of his working life, he invested in the stock market—every dollar he saved. After thirty years of doing this, he had grown his portfolio to $2.5 million. Now, I'm not recommending that you live on $35,000 per annum, and I'm not telling you to take all your savings and plow it into the stock market. But doing either or even both of these things is better than spending all your income. The fellow who came calling on me was blessed with both discipline *and* luck. He is also an example of this truth: There are no excuses when you want to amass a respectable amount of wealth. You must be highly disciplined in your saving habits and in your investing habits. It is this discipline that will get you to the point of financial freedom. You can't say to yourself: *When I make $300,000, $500,000, or $1 million dollars a year, I will start saving and investing.* You must start saving and investing now to build the future that you envision. No excuses!

Never Underestimate the Cost of the Lifestyle You Have and the Lifestyle You Want

As you march through the process of understanding what your lifestyle costs, it's very important not to underestimate your expenses. Yet most people do just that. Shortfalls tend to derail your plans, and that imperils your future. In my own experience, many clients underestimate their expenses by 10 to 20 percent. This can be lethal to the outcome you are planning on. The success of your plan is proportional to the effort you spend researching your expenses and analyzing them over time. Examine the past twelve months under a microscope. Then look even farther back. This is the only way to understand your spending trends. Begin by determining precisely what you spend in a year's time. The object is neither to pat yourself on the back or beat yourself up. It is to make best, most thoroughly informed financial decisions possible.

How do people go wrong? I find that many of my clients simply forget to include such expenditures as gifts for children and grandchildren throughout the year. All those birthdays and holidays add up. So can maintenance expenses for your home, extra vacations, servicing your cars, unexpected medical expenses, and charitable gifts. Overlook nothing. If you are left with some "unknowns" in your debit column, at least put a dollar amount on them. Look, there's no way anyone can predict exactly what circumstances will happen and what those things will cost in the coming year. The closest you can come is to account for your spending history, determine the predictable outlays, and base your future planning on these.

If you are a business owner, there is another common source of underestimated expenses. Most owners pass quite a few expenses through their business accounts. To calculate your work-optional lifestyle costs correctly, you must figure all these business expenses into what will become added personal expenses. Most of my business-owning clients pass through their business as much as a third (or even more) of their overall lifestyle costs. When these business-owner clients create their plan of action, they all too often forget to add these expenses back into their calculation. Remember to add everything, and then leave room for the unknowns.

Accounting for the Future

I always tell my clients that estimating lifestyle costs is the one area in financial planning that requires the greatest precision. It is crucial that you factor into your plan every last penny. On the other hand, don't drive yourself into paranoia and paralysis. One of the more reassuring principles I pass along is that whatever your expenses have been over the past twenty years and whatever lifestyle you have been living during that period, dramatic change is unlikely. This prediction requires neither an advanced degree in economics nor a crystal ball. It is valid simply because you are accustomed to this way of living and spending. Your current lifestyle is largely a matter of habit. one that you're accustomed to living. True, as you contemplate retirement or work-optional living, you will be entering a new phase in your life. This does not have to entail a radical change in your spending habits— say an uptick of 20 to 30 percent. I can tell you this based on more than twenty years of experience in financial planning. Overwhelmingly, my clients spend post-work pretty much at the same rate that they spent while they were working. Thus, the more accurate the picture you have of your spending level and the more complete grasp of the costs of maintaining your lifestyle after you walk away from your job, the greater the likelihood that you will be able to live out the vision you have for your life.

Once you diligently complete this exacting self-accounting process, you will emerge with a much clearer picture of what you are going to need per year.

Now, turn to the future. Go through every line item and ask yourself: *Will this expense continue going forward? If so, for how long?*

For example, if you have a mortgage or an equity line on your primary or secondary residence, will you still carry that mortgage? If so, for how long? Perhaps you have a plan in place to pay off the mortgage at a specific time. Alternatively, new expenses may be added as time moves forward. For example, during your full-time career, you may have taken only one or two vacations per year because you didn't have the time to be out of town longer. Now, you are free to take three or four. This perk of your new freedom is not free of cost. Take the new expenses into account before you finalize your calculations.

There is certainly much unpredictability in life. Maximize the overall predictability of your life by accurately accounting for *predictable* changes in expenses. Include the decreases as well as the increases. Both changes will affect your overall plan and how you execute it. Predict the impact as accurately as you can. Do it now.

The last step in the process of expenditure review is to calculate the impact of inflation on your expenses over the next five, ten, or twenty years. Ben Franklin famously said that the only two certainties in life were death and taxes. We could all be forgiven if we decided to add a third: inflation. The lives of most of us, from Baby Boomers to Gen Z-ers, have lived with it. Yet a lot of people omit inflation from their long-term financial management plan. That is a mistake. You should calculate how inflation will likely increase each of your expenses over the coming five, ten, or twenty years. Consider: The top four expense items that make up the greatest percentage of total spending are housing, healthcare, transportation, and food/beverages—in that order. From 1982 through 2020, these expenses have increased significantly due to inflation, on average from 2.7% to 4.7% annually.

Of course, unknowns can suddenly arrive front and center. Most recently, Covid-19 has triggered exceptional inflation. Inflation has been higher in the wake of this pandemic than in more than forty years, with over 8 percent in the US during September 2022. How long such inflation will last is almost impossible to say, but it is likely that we will see inflation numbers higher than what we have been accustomed to over the past twenty years. Here's a simple example for you to be thinking about. The Rule of 72 is a popular rule of thumb formula used to estimate the number of years required to double invested money at a given annual rate of return. We can also apply it to calculate the impact of inflation on your expenses. Say inflation averages 4 percent per year and you are spending $200,000 per year. Apply the Rule of 72, we find that your current $200,000 package of expenses will double in eighteen years to $400,000.

Clearly, it is critical to factor inflation into your financial analysis and planning. It is also clear that making these inflation adjustments in your head is pretty much impossible. There are so many moving parts that a concrete visualization of the data is mandatory.

HOW TO GO BROKE WITH $20,000,000 IN YOUR HIP POCKET

Let's begin with some good news and then follow up with a cautionary tale.

The good news is that, as we grow older, some of our expenses will be reduced. For instance, maybe you're not able or inclined to take multiple vacations per year, even though you had planned to. So, you stay home more often. Maybe you find that you enjoy cooking at home, now that you have the time for it. So, you no longer spend as much eating out multiple times per week. Perhaps, with an empty nest, you and your spouse feel like you're rattling around in too much house, and you decide to downsize to something cozier and easier and cheaper to maintain. This could well add funds to your portfolio—not just in money saved but, depending on the state of the real estate market in your area, in money gained. There is research that suggests your expenses may well decline from the ages sixty-four to seventy-five and beyond by approximately 25 to 30 percent. From my experience, I don't believe that to be exactly true. It is factual that when you move into an advanced age, say eighty years and older, you may not be able to travel and dine out as often, so yes, these are costly expenses that will be reduced. Furthermore, if you are active at a country club playing golf, tennis or now pickleball, again, you may not be able to participate in these activities. So, perhaps you may decide to cancel your membership. However, with these expenses being reduced or eliminated, healthcare costs may fill the gap. I typically reduce my clients' overall expenses by approximately 10-15% at the age of eighty-five years old when I analyze their financial plan. This is significant and should be factored into your plan, even if only as part of an if/then scenario.

Now for the cautionary tale. A prospective client came to me after hearing one of my lectures. He said he was "deeply concerned about running out of money in retirement."

"How much money do you have now?" was the logical first question to ask, and I asked it.

"$20 million," he replied.

I wanted to respond with something like "How can someone with $20 million be worried about running out of money?" But I bit my tongue and asked him a far more relevant and useful question: "Exactly how much money are you spending per year?"

"Eight hundred thousand," he replied. Then added "net."

The *net* was a significant piece of data. I quickly ran the numbers in my head and concluded, depending on his tax rate and which accounts he planned on withdrawing his income from, a million to a million-point-two or more is what he would need to withdraw to come up with an after-tax net figure of $800,000.

I was glad I hadn't asked him the first question that crossed my mind because it was instantly easy to see that his concern was legitimate. Withdrawing $1 million from a $20 million portfolio represents a 5 percent annual withdrawal. This individual was just fifty-two years old, so he needed to plan for many more years of life. His 5 percent withdrawal rate put him at a high probability of running out of money before he ran out of life. Statistics derived from the research on withdrawal rates tell us that the greater your withdrawal rate, the greater the chance that you will run out of money.

I will go into the significance of this kind of calculation later in the book, but what you need to know now is that you may have $500,000 or $50 million. Either way, understanding your expenses and how much you are spending is critical to your ability to maintain your lifestyle without running out of fuel.

Not surprisingly, I have noticed that the more money people make or accumulate, the more their lifestyle costs them. I mean, it is easy to think to yourself that I now *make a million per year, so when I go on vacation, I can book a suite that is double the cost of the room I used to book before I made a million.* You may even say out loud, "I'm going to give my wardrobe a $20,000 upgrade." Or, "I'm getting that car because I can handle a monthly payment of two grand."

Financial planning is not just about how much money you have on hand or how much you make. It is also about what your lifestyle costs are going to be. So far as financial planning goes, the significance of what's in the bank, what's in your investment portfolio, and what's in your paycheck is not absolute but relative to the cost of your lifestyle.

Whatever your assets, there is one question you must ask yourself when making a purchase: *Do I need this or do I want this?*

If you determine that the need is actually a want, ask yourself a follow-up question: *How will buying this change my life?* In other words, will acquiring this item really make you feel that much better about yourself? Just because you have worked hard to be able to make this "want-to-have" purchase doesn't oblige you to act on the impulse to buy it. Even if you feel you are wealthy enough to squander your money, is it a good idea to do so?

You can make informed predictions about the future. That is what wealth management is all about. But no one can know what will actually happen tomorrow. Those stories you hear about very wealthy people who lose everything? Well, at least some of them are true. I have known such people. Understanding your lifestyle is fundamental to understanding where you stand now and deciding if you have amassed sufficient assets to generate an income to support you and your family in the lifestyle you want. Live your life with a plan, combine that plan with humility, and be as smart as possible in every decision that you make.

CHAPTER 5

INCOME SOURCES

Only after you have a full picture of your lifestyle expenses are you prepared to meaningfully ask three key questions about your sources of income:

1. How will I be able to pay for these lifestyle expenses?

2. What uncertainties and risks will I have to be thinking about along the way?

3. What else do I need to prepare for?

With my clients, I approach the answers to these questions by framing them in the seven main risks that everyone must recognize and understand when they are formulating a financial plan.

Planning for the Unknown: The Seven Risks

1. **Longevity Risk**. The most obvious risk is that you will outlive your portfolio, which is especially a concern for those who have a family history of longevity. For a couple who are both

sixty-five years old, there is a 25 percent chance that one of them will live past ninety-five. This amounts to more than a thirty-year retirement time horizon!

2. **Solvency Risk**. Unfortunately, the problem with government and employer income sources should be a concern for retirees. Social Security and Medicare are in a precarious financial position that may force them to reduce benefits over time. As for pension plans, benefit reductions or outright defaults are distressingly common.

3. **Savings Risk**. Most people are just not saving enough for a work-optional lifestyle.

4. **Inflation Risk**. The problem with inflation is that it erodes the value of your savings and reduces your return. To combat the frequently extreme fluctuations of the stock market, retirement portfolios are sometimes weighted more toward fixed-income investments. The problem is that conservative investments paying a fixed income are not always capable of keeping pace with inflation. Take note that, for certain expense categories, inflation can become significantly higher than the core (overall) inflation rate. For example, healthcare inflation has averaged 4.7% annually over the time (1982-2020, J.P. Morgan).

5. **Market Volatility Risk**. When an investment market or even a particular security undergoes periods of unpredictable, sharp movements in price, the situation is said to be volatile. Market Volatility can cause portfolio values to fluctuate, moving both up and down. If the market drops or if corrections (a "correction" occurs when a stock index declines more than 10

percent from a recent high) occur early in your work-optional phase, your portfolio may not provide sufficient cushion to absorb the added stress of systematic withdrawals you may be taking for income purposes. This can diminish the portfolio to a point where it will not provide the income necessary to maintain your desired lifestyle. Ultimately, the portfolio may run out of money, and you may have to scramble to reallocate your investments.

6. **Spending Risk.** As discussed in Chapter 5, understanding your expenses is critical to planning. To mitigate or minimize your spending risk, you need to carefully assess, with respect to lifestyle, what needs are essential versus those of lower priority and scale your spending and spending habits accordingly.

7. **Withdrawal Risk**: Everyone needs qualified financial guidance on withdrawal rates and what may be sustainable over a long work-optional period span. This is also true for the sequence of withdrawals and required minimum distributions (RMDs) that are made from your tax-deferred accounts. You need a strategy that balances the need to satisfy RMD requirements without incurring unnecessary capital gains taxes on excessively large withdrawals. It can be a sensitive wealth management issue.

Understanding and planning for all seven risks should be a top-of-mind priority as you lay out your plan for achieving a work-optional lifestyle.

Potential Sources of Income

Despite the very real impact of the seven risks, including the volatility of securities markets, you have many potential sources of more predictable fixed income to consider in building your financial plan. Some of the most common fixed sources are these:

- real estate properties (producing rental and lease income)
- income from your business or multiple businesses
- income from your portfolio (which includes your non-retirement accounts and retirement accounts)
- pension plan
- Social Security

Compared to the others, the last two sources on this list play a much smaller role in what you bring in, but they still count as a percentage of your total income. I mentioned earlier that my grandfather retired from Con Ed as a boiler worker when he was sixty-two. In 1992, he was dependent on a pension and his Social Security check for 80 percent of his retirement income. The remainder came from a few dividends derived from a small holding in Con Ed stock. While he was working, my grandfather saved $0.25 per paycheck and bought Con Ed stock, which ended up growing to a value of $300,000 by the time he retired. Con Ed was paying a dividend of 5 percent, which provided $15,000 in extra income per year. Today, Social Security and pensions are estimated to make up 37 percent of most people's income needs.

Sources of Retirement Income

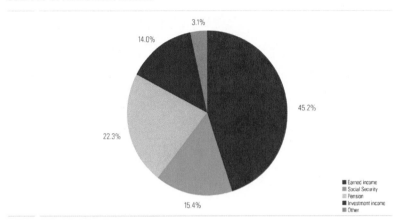

This is a very different situation from that of my grandfather and so many others thirty years ago.

Additionally, Social Security is now under great strain because there are more beneficiaries per every 100 workers. When President Franklin D. Roosevelt signed the Social Security Act in 1935, the nation was in the depths of the Great Depression. As reported in The Social Security Administration's *Annual Report of the Board of Trustees of the Federal Old Age and Survivors Insurance and Disability Insurance Trust Funds, 2020,* the ratio of workers to beneficiaries was much higher than it is today: 41.9 workers to 1 beneficiary. By the year 2035, estimates put this ratio at 2.2 workers to 1 beneficiary. Dependence on Social Security and pensions is likely headed for drastic reductions as we go forward.

The takeaway message here is that you must assume that more of the responsibility for generating the necessary income to unlock your own work-optional lifestyle will rest chiefly on your shoulders. For this reason, among others, no matter how much money you earn, you must remain diligent in saving and investing in risk assets capable of building a large enough nest egg to fund your retirement for many long-lived years.

CHAPTER 6

MAKING THE WORK-OPTIONAL TRANSITION

After spending two decades working for some of the largest Wall Street banks, I finally decided to start my own independent financial firm. With this transition, I became a business owner rather than an employee. Changing from working for someone else to starting my own firm was exhilarating as well as eye-opening. When I look back on that time, I can only say that the experience changed something in my soul that drove me forward with a completely new level of energy to devote to my work.

At long last, I could say: *This firm is mine and mine only*! But the most important benefit of starting this company was that I became a better wealth manager to my clients. The reason for this was simple. I was no longer serving two masters—my corporate bosses (who were themselves serving the company's shareholders) and my clients. I was serving my clients and only my clients. I was a genuine fiduciary, legally required to put their needs above my own. I thrived in this arrangement.

Beyond this, owning my firm offered incredible economic benefits that positioned me to go after that same work optional-lifestyle I was advocating for my clients. Once I realized that I had made it to the point where work was optional for me, I felt a wave of calm, peace, and well-being wash over me. It moved me to revise my website to focus my mission on helping my clients achieve peace of mind. The ultimate source of this serenity and satisfaction came with working toward and achieving a work-optional lifestyle. To this day, I want others to experience the same feeling I have. It makes the work I do—I *choose* to do—no less arduous but much more meaningful for my clients as well as for me.

My business is helping people invest in their future security, happiness, and freedom. There is another dimension as well. I have always admired my wife's family. She comes from a background of multigenerational business owners, who inherited their dad's business, which they took to a whole new level. To me, this is a special form of business success. I have three sons of my own, and I am betting that at least one of them will want to take the reins of my company one day. I would love to create a situation like that of my wife's family, in which my household will be the heart of a multigenerational business. It is my dream to be that portrait on the wall to which my children and, God willing, grandchildren can point and say: *That's the guy who started Palumbo Wealth Management.* That very thought is sufficient to create a level of energy and excitement in me that I never imagined before opening my own firm.

At the same time that I see myself as having created what has the potential of being a multi-generational enterprise, I am also completely confident that I could sell my firm tomorrow and walk away from it. Between my personal savings and investments, I would be free never to worry about working again.

Create the Life You Want, Live the Life You Create

As important as the knowledge of my freedom is to me, walking away from work is not the vision I have for my life. I love the work I do, and I want to continue having a major positive impact on the lives of my clients while I establish a strong legacy for my three sons—if they want it. Yes, for me, work is now optional. I've achieved that goal, and I am free to step away at any time. It's just that I can't imagine life without my work because I'm passionate about what I do.

Starting your own business gives you the ability to build something with unlimited possibility. Most people who set out to do so understand on some level that this is the only way they'll ever have full control over their own future, their life's journey. When you own your own business, you never have to answer to anyone. Ever. You never have to worry about walking into an office one day, being called in by your supervisor or manager, and getting fired.

Talk about risk! Most of us grow up thinking that the surest path to job security is found through working for others. Big corporations seem like fortresses, and it's better to be inside looking out than outside looking in. It's good to be an employee!

But the reality is that employees are living high-risk lives, and just because so many others live the same way doesn't make the risk any less real. As an employee, you trade a large measure of freedom for nothing more than the feeling of having a secure job. Worse, your family is obliged to make the same compromise as you have made.

Of course, there are risks to owning your own business. But the risks, I believe, are greater when you relinquish so much control to others. You are the decision maker. You have direct control over your destiny. You have an array of options, and you are free to invent even more. Besides, there are tax advantages that are simply unavailable to employees, and these are invaluable to helping you grow your wealth. The less you pay in taxes, the more you bring home to save and invest. Moreover, you have the ability to sell your business on your terms and the option to have a family member run the business while you live off the income stream. No wonder being a business owner is the fastest way to unlock the work-optional lifestyle for yourself. It gives you a wealth of opportunities to create the life you want.

Find Your Passion, Own Your Passion

Tax advantages, building *real* job security, and creating a family legacy are all great reasons for becoming a business owner. But you need to find passion in whatever you choose to do with your career. Find something that excites you so much that you can't wait to get out of bed and go to work. You must discover a career that drives you to continue finding ways to continually become better at what you do. Maybe for you, it's about helping and making a difference for your clients. Maybe it's about creating new branches and opportunities for your company to expand and create opportunities for your employees.

Whatever it is that absorbs you, I cannot overstate the importance of thinking about how you can help others. Of course, there are economic benefits to you in serving others, but if you do not have the mindset to be helpful to others in a service business, you are not going to succeed and you will not derive the profound gratification of knowing you made a difference in someone's life.

> *If you are not making a difference in someone's life, you are wasting your time.*

I think about this sentence daily. Yes, I'm a financial planner and a wealth manager, and I think money is a great thing and the freedom it brings is even greater, but money truly is not and can never be everything. If money is your only driver, you will not achieve the high degree of success you and your family deserve.

I will never forget a wonderful client of mine who ran a very successful business importing Asian grocery goods. He ran a $25 million operation and was absolutely on top of his game.

"How did you become so successful?" I asked him.

"Phil, I have a tremendous passion for what I do. I never fully expected it to turn into all of this, but I knew it was possible. I just focused on the day-to-day task ahead, and the money followed me. I didn't chase money; I just love my job." Find something you love, do it with passion, and the odds are high that the money will follow.

Ask yourself what it feels like to have a true passion for what you do. Think about it for a moment. This is often an epiphany moment for my clients. It's powerful when they can imagine loving their jobs and fully enjoying their day-to-day lives. I remember working at Merrill Lynch, which was my first firm right out of college. Every day, I reported to my desk and sat in my cubicle for hours on end. After working there for just three months, I was sitting in my cubicle one evening around seven like normal. I looked around and it just hit me, what my life had at this point become. In that exact moment, I had my own epiphany. I knew I was going to be a wealth manager for the rest of my life. From that moment on, I spent my free time studying for the several exams that I had to take to convert my epiphany into my reality and become a financial advisor.

That instinctive moment of insight is beyond explanation. I just feel lucky to have experienced it while I was still very new to my career. So many people end up going through their careers without ever really enjoying what they're doing. This is a shame, maybe even a tragedy. After all, we spend at least a third of our lives "at work."

It's an old story, and it's about time to change the narrative. What if you woke up every morning knowing that you are in a position to walk away from your job for whatever reason you wanted? Maybe you feel like going part-time so that you can chase other endeavors. What if you could? Perhaps you want to start a new venture. What if that were possible? If you feel the urge to travel the world for a year, could you? Or retiring "early"—possible?

With timely planning, it is all within reach. And it can open a wonderful way to go through this journey we call life. You may enjoy sitting at a desk all day. But no one wants to be chained to it. We all have mornings when we don't much feel like going to work. But no one wants to wake up every day regretting that they have to go to work.

You owe it to yourself and your family to think about this on a deeper level. Let's look at where you are right now in life. Are you fulfilled and happy in what you do for a living? Or is there a different career path you want to explore? Do you want, really want, to start your own business?

I am not saying that it is impossible to be fulfilled working for someone else. I am saying that doing so is not the fastest, most direct route to a work-optional lifestyle. One-size-fits-all can be disappointing or downright painful as a way to live your life. You have only one life, and if your dreams do not currently coincide with your reality, you are the only one who can make those dreams real.

The work or career we choose has a tremendous impact on our happiness. Yes, making more money reduces our need to worry about money, and that surely contributes to happiness. But satisfaction with the work you do is rarely all about money. Your work is one of the things that defines who you are. Who you serve and who you help— these give your work value beyond money.

An old-time manager at Merrill Lynch once gave us a tremendous talk that made me want to sit down with him and pick his brain. So, we sat down together, and I went through my entire strategy for growing my practice *within* Merrill Lynch. He told me that my plan sounded good to him and that, "I outlined all the right things." Then he pulled open his desk drawer, took out a yellow pad, ripped out a piece of paper from it, took a pen from his pocket, and drew the Nike swoosh sign on it. He looked straight at me.

"JUST DO IT!" he said.

Taking the Risk

Although I have learned that owning your own business provides greater security as well as a faster route to a work-optional life, leaving a major Wall Street bank does call for a certain level of courage and conviction. You are leaving the familiar for the new, and there are risks. I have a family that's made up of my lovely wife and three amazing boys. When I left the company, I was contractually bound not to bring any client information out the door. I was able to utilize old information that I had from previous firms I worked at, which was helpful in contacting some of my clients. I put everything on the line, and yes, could have lost everything…everything I had worked so hard for over the first half of my career. So much could have gone wrong—but it didn't. I had a deep conviction that the decision I made to start my independent financial firm was the right decision for myself and for my clients. Even though I couldn't solicit some of my former clients, as I embarked on this journey, I had a strong belief that many of them would seek *me* out.

I am glad I saw it through and I am grateful for my family's support as I ended up retaining 96% of my clients, which was simply amazing. All of us are on the path toward financial independence. Why *wouldn't* they want to come on board? I had experienced firsthand the fiduciary conflict inherent in having a wealth manager who answers to a company and shareholders first and clients second. I had spent twenty years protecting my clients from these conflicts, which was almost a job in itself. Instead of having to be distracted by this, I was now creating an environment where all my work focused on my clients exclusively. I was able to provide them with the best service possible. I wanted my firm to be more personal while cultivating great relationships with each human being who walked through the door. Over time, I know that I executed that strategic goal to the very best of my ability. My team and I are only getting better as we continue to grow and learn together. If you want to build something great in life, if you truly have the desire to optimize every skillset you have, take a lesson from my Merrill Lynch manager: *JUST DO IT!*

CHAPTER 7

WHY A FINANCIAL PLAN IS IMPORTANT

Looking back at what we've discussed so far, let's take a moment to review and analyze. We've covered the concept of creating a vision for your life, today and going forward; the need to know what assets you've accumulated up to this point (real estate holdings, businesses, portfolio assets, and cash value from life insurance and retirement accounts) and the need to understand your own lifestyle cost. This cost is the number your assets have to meet or, even better, significantly exceed.

When I ask people to dive deeper into these topics, the anxiety is sometimes palpable. The linked ideas of financial planning and personal analysis have been around for years, but there is a yawning gulf between understanding and doing. Most people who come into my office or who talk to me outside, do not have in hand a formal financial analysis.

Why not? Fear. A lot of people are afraid to look into the details.

So, they make reflexive defensive excuses.

It's not necessary, Phil.

My plan is in my head.

I know what I need to do.

My answer to these deflections is always, yes, you can go through your entire life without a financial plan and end up okay. Just understand that you are putting yourself steps ahead of the game if you create, record, and study a full analysis. Simply taking the time to work up an organized document that showcases the details of your financial situation will do wonders for easing—if not totally eliminating—anxiety and doubt. Believe me, it is the *not* knowing that causes the most fear. There is much truth in the biblical verse the CIA adopted as its motto: "And ye shall know the truth, and the truth will set you free." When you see what needs to be done, you can build conviction and confidence in your future. You can put yourself in the position of managing your income streams so that you can see ahead and be confident that you will not run out of money. You will understand how much money you can safely spend each month. Most importantly, you will give yourself a better chance to maximize wealth throughout your lifetime.

Creating a Blueprint

Just as an architect designing a home first draws it out on paper or a computer screen, you can draw out your life right before your eyes. Make the trajectory of your finances so clearly visible that you can see all the details. In this way, you know what changes, both small and large, will set you up for success. Believe me when I tell you that this visualization is ultimately a straightforward task and will make a tremendous difference in your ability to maximize your accrued wealth over time.

This is exactly what having a financial plan is all about! It is not mysterious. Quite the contrary, it solves the mystery. It is not intended to shame, embarrass, scold, discourage, or otherwise to create stress but to do the opposite. It will lift you to a greater understanding of your situation and point the way toward optimizing it.

The fear that stops many people from building financial plans is the dread that they didn't save enough money and invest properly and that it is too late to start now. They believe that revealing this in actual numbers makes it true, putting the last nail in their financial coffin. In reality, such fear stifles success. While it is true that the earlier you start planning, the better, who is to say that it is ever too late to make at least some positive impact?

Financial fear of knowing is not restricted to those of modest means. Some of the bigger financial players are the most reluctant to see their net worth set forth in numbers. That makes it real, and they are in no hurry to recognize reality.

High Withdrawal Rates Will Quickly Deplete Your Assets
Simulated Portfolio Values (90% confidence level)

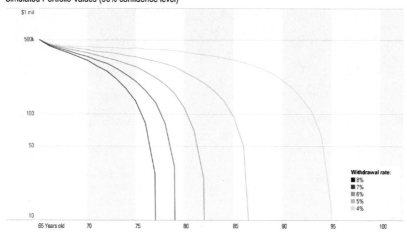

IMPORTANT: Projections generated by Morningstar regarding the likelihood of various investment outcomes using the Ibbotson Wealth Forecasting Engine are hypothetical in nature, do not reflect actual investment results, and are not guarantees of future results. Results may vary over time and with each simulation. This is for illustrative purposes only and not indicative of any investment. An investment cannot be made directly in an index. © Morningstar 2022 and Precision Information, dba Financial Fitness Group 2022. All Rights Reserved.

A while back, I mentioned the impact of withdrawal rates on your money supply. The danger is significant and often overlooked, especially by people who do not perform a financial analysis and make a financial plan. Take a look at the example in this chart.

If you stopped working at sixty-five and withdrew your savings at an annual rate of 8 percent, you could run out of money by the time you are seventy-six or seventy-seven. Compare this to someone who takes a withdrawal of 4 percent. They enjoy a high probability that their money will last until they are ninety-five years old. You can't know your withdrawal rate unless you analyze your spending versus your income streams, your assets, and your saving rate.

ANALYSIS AND SIMULATION

Now that we've gone through the importance of making and applying a personal financial plan, let's tackle the details. We are well past the era of pencil and paper. An array of software solutions is available to make our financial calculations and analysis much more accurate. Technology facilitates your ability to analyze your lifestyle to determine if you are at the point where work has become optional or when you will reach that point. Today, the range and sophistication of financial planning software is greater than ever. I frequently say that anyone can input data into a software program, but skilled students of financial planning understand how to interpret the data in a way that's strikingly comprehensible. The most commonly used analytical approach in financial software is the Monte Carlo Simulation, a digitized mathematical technique that allows users to account for risk-taking within the bounds of quantitative analysis and decision-making. Input the data, and the software furnishes the decision maker with a range of possible outcomes, along with the probability of a given outcome occurring in a given circumstance.

The Monte Carlo simulation is not a substitute for human judgment and imagination—thinking is always required in financial planning—but is nevertheless extraordinarily useful as a tool to aid in determining where you stand today and if your vision for tomorrow can become reality. Each Monte Carlo simulation stress tests your financial situation one thousand times to produce hard data that can give you great confidence that you are either on track or not. The stress tests account for the assets you have saved, how you've invested those assets, and your lifestyle costs. They also assume that you will live to be ninety-five years old since the last thing you want is to make a financial plan that throws you to the wolves if you happen to have the "misfortune" of longevity.

The genius of the Monte Carlo software is that it "knows" that, from a return and risk standpoint, your investment outcomes will vary; therefore, the only way to increase the accuracy of predictions is to stress test the various outcomes a thousand times. Your investments may return 7 percent this year, producing a certain level of risk, but perhaps -5 percent the following year, and so on. Analysis that takes this inevitable variation into account is much better than simply inputting data into Excel in a straight linear approach that assumes your investments earn 7 percent a year forecasting until ninety-five years. Many people use this static technique, but such linear financial projections are inherently flawed because they do not factor in the risks you are taking over time, the risk embodied in the variation in your returns year after year. In a stress-tested Monte Carlo Simulation, the variation risk is central, and that means the results of the simulation will be as accurate as possible in the absence of a crystal ball. One hundred percent accuracy? Of course not, but there is plenty of data that you can use and stress test to create a substantial variety of what-if scenarios that accurately reflect the real world. Having an array of iterations legitimately builds confidence in your planning for getting from where you stand today to where you want to stand—in a place from which work truly becomes optional.

I wish I could say that the keyword here is CERTAINTY. But it *certainly* is not. I can tell you that the accurate keyword is CONFIDENCE because you know that your financial situation has been stress-tested a thousand times, a predictive technique that has a record of great success. This should earn you a high degree of financial peace of mind.

Confidence Is a Matter of Levels

The accompanying chart reveals a range of confidence levels, expressed in terms of percentages, that your proposed plan will succeed in getting you to work optional by a desired point.

Interpreting Confidence Levels in Simulation

Confidence level	Chance of exceeding	Chance of falling short
50%	50%	50%
75%	75%	25%
90% (More conservative)	90%	10%

This table is intended to help interpret 50%, 75%, and 90% confidence levels illustrated in the following images. © Morningstar 2022 and Precision Information, dba Financial Fitness Group 2022. All Rights Reserved.

In any financial analysis, you want to be as conservative as possible. A confidence level of 50 percent or even 75 percent is unacceptable. We should aim for our plans to produce an outcome that reaches a 90 to 95 percent confidence level or even greater. The more conservative you are, the higher the probability that you will *not* run out of money before you meet your maker. This confidence all starts with a thoughtful, data-based, and stress-tested financial plan. Remember, anyone can input data into a software program, but a competent financial planner has the knowledge and experience to interpret this data correctly, based on a plausible variety of what-if scenarios

The first what-if scenario I use is what I call the *current scenario.* It shows you where you stand today, how your money is invested, the projected rate of return on each of your investment categories, and what your overall confidence level is right now. This scenario assumes inflation of 2 percent and dives deeper into each topic of analysis. I consider this your first data point, and it is a check that your current scenario yields a confidence level greater than 90 percent—in other words, tells you that you have a nine in ten chance of not running out of money before the age of ninety-five.

As a second data point, we rerun the current scenario with things that could set your plan off-track a bit. Let's say inflation averages 4 percent moving forward. If that were to happen, where would your confidence level be? Would it now stay at 90 percent or above? Or would it drop down to 70-75 percent? This is extremely important because we know that inflation has been as high as 14 percent back in the 1970s and early 1980s. Any number of things can happen to send your plan off track.

Let's say a client retired in 1970 and then lived through an extremely high inflation rate for the next fourteen years. This upended his entire financial plan. Such an occurrence is obviously a possibility. We know this because it has actually happened. While we cannot predict the future with absolute accuracy, we can look at current data, which tells us that inflation could possibly become as bad as it was in the 1970s and early 1980s, which is a rate much higher than what we've been accustomed to over the past twenty years. (PS: Not being aware of or ignoring this possibility will *not* make you immune to it!)

The third data point of interest focuses on your income. In the first scenario, let's assume you want to spend x amount of dollars in income per year. Based on that figure, you have a 90 percent-plus confidence level. I use this third data point to show clients the maximum amount they can spend and continue living at a confidence level of 90 percent or more. For example, if your income needs are set at $200,000 per year in your current scenario, and you have a 90 percent level of confidence, you may find out that you actually have $250,000 to spend. The reason why I like to share this with my clients is not to give them the green light to go ahead and spend $250,000 but to show them that some wiggle room is available—*if needed*. That said, I always encourage my clients to lean toward the conservative approach.

The fourth data point is, I would argue, the most important. It is to take all the data we input and then assume the investment return on your portfolio will average 3 percent moving forward. I suggest this conservative estimate because it gives us room for changes in response to various outcomes. Absent a functioning crystal ball, we cannot predict the future with certainty. We cannot tell you with anything like perfect accuracy the rate of return by which your personal portfolio will grow over time. There is no way to guarantee that everything will work as planned, from the moment we make the plan to and through your eighties, nineties, and quite possibly beyond. This may sound obvious, and it *should* be obvious. Too often, however, financial firms furnish optimistic numerical data that is too confident. This inflation of confidence comes not because a particular financial advisor likes you and wants you to feel good but because he's trying to sell you his plan.

My conservative approach avoids a wishful emphasis on the best case. This doesn't mean I focus on the worst-case outcome, either. Instead, I take a pragmatic and conservative look at the foundation of the client's portfolio. From the perspective of 2022, the past ten years have shown investment returns that were abnormally high. When you are going through a financial planning process, you don't want to fall into the trap of assuming the exceptional will inevitably continue. Instead, it is best to ensure that the investment-return assumptions you make are conservative. That is why I begin by reviewing with my clients a forecasted return of just 3 percent on their portfolio, assuming they live to age ninety-five. If this assumption gets their Monte Carlo simulations to high confidence that they will realize their vision, then I advise them that they do not need to be as aggressive moving forward. At this rate of growth, you don't need to incur the risks that come with investing in securities that offer higher rates—and the volatility that goes with them. Less volatility means fewer worries. When you get to the work-optional point, you will find that you can afford to walk away from employment without sacrificing your lifestyle, even if your money goes down by 50 percent. Remember: the goal is not work-optional *if you are lucky and everything goes exactly according to plan.* It is work-optional even if life throws you some curveballs (as life tends to do).

The final data point is what I call the *sequence of returns.* This addresses a situation in which you happen to walk away from work during the same period in which the economy goes into a recession, producing negative market returns during a two-to-three- year period.

How will this affect your end-all scenario? Will you run out of money before running out of life?

For example, let's say you retired in March of 2000, and the S&P 500 declined 47 percent from its peak on March 24 of that year to the trough on October 8, 2002. In addition, from March 29, 2000, the S&P 500 traded at 1508 and on February 6, 2013, traded at 1512, so it was essentially flat for some thirteen years. Obviously, this scenario would not lead to the best outcome for someone who has just stopped working. Or let's say you stopped working in January 2010, at the height of a tremendous bull market that sent the S&P 500 up 326 percent by the end of 2021. My point? It is imperative to stress-test your plan in the light of all plausible scenarios and make sure that you are in a comfortable position despite the array of adversity you may encounter.

A similar example to these is shown here.

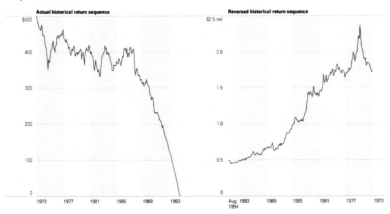

The Sequence of Returns Can Significantly Affect Your Retirement
Sequence of Returns Matters

It illustrates the value of $500,000 invested at the beginning of 1973, assuming an inflation-adjusted withdrawal rate of 5 percent in a 50/50 stock and bond portfolio. The value of your portfolio drops to zero by 1994. Take the same scenario but change the retirement year to 1994, and you get a much different outcome. This illustrates a basic reversal of the historical return sequence, ending with your money being worth over $1.5 million. The order and timing of poor investment returns can make a huge impact on how long your retirement savings will last.

While we cannot predict the future with 100 percent certainty, we are certainly able to analyze an array of scenarios and provide sufficient clarity to place high confidence in conservative investment and savings. It is crucial to avoid countering a disappointing analysis by taking on more risk. That is, if analysis of your plan shows that you will run out of money, your first impulse may be to take on more risk with investments that offer higher returns.

Probability of Meeting Income Needs
Various Withdrawal Rates and Portfolio Allocations Over a 25-year Retirement

84%	97%	95%	92%	87%	4% Withdrawal rate
28%	69%	79%	79%	77%	5%
3%	26%	54%	63%	65%	6%
0%	4%	29%	46%	52%	7%
0%	0%	12%	29%	40%	8%
100% Bonds	75% B 25% S	50% B 50% S	25% B 75% S	100% Stocks	■ 76%–100% ■ 51%–75% □ 26%–50% □ 0%–25%

PALUMBO
WEALTH MANAGEMENT

The accompanying chart, however, shows that the more risk you assume, the lower the predictability, so as you can see by reviewing the chart, your probability of running out of money actually increases. When you take more risks with your investments, your portfolio becomes highly volatile. A volatile portfolio is more challenging to forecast. Consider this simple example: if you invest in a twenty-year CD that pays an interest of 3 percent, you can be certain of how much money you will earn from the CD every year for two decades. If you take that same amount of money and invest in stocks, you have no idea of the outcome twenty years from now. You may average 5 percent per year or even 18 percent per year. Or much less. The outcomes depend on many factors, which multiply the volatility of the investment.

My goal in running multiple scenarios with multiple stat points is to take my clients through the range of likely outcomes and thus present as many options as possible. Don't just hope to avoid adverse economic forces. Prepare for them by arming yourself with the information and knowledge that will enable you to build conviction and confidence for your next steps. This is how to get to the point where you can unlock a work-optional lifestyle without worrying about your money. It doesn't happen by writing steps or notes on the back of an envelope. It doesn't happen by formulating a "plan" in your head or by thinking about it at the kitchen table with the aid of a calculator. Making a true plan takes dedication, thought, and thorough analysis. To get to where you want to go, you need a full understanding of where you are today.

CHAPTER 8

HOW TO INVEST YOUR MONEY

After showing my clients their financial plan for the first time, I always tell them that the correct follow-up question should be: "Phil, this sounds great, but how are you going to manage my money to make sure that I can achieve this vision?"

Good question, if I do say so myself. You can have access to the best technology, all the pretty charts, and a wealth of information necessary to analyze a client's financial situation, but the engine that's going to drive their success is the investment strategy itself. When I'm going through the financial planning process with a client and analyzing the details of their situation, these are the simple questions *I* ask:

- What is your specific number?
- What's the amount that you need each month to live?
- What do you have to have each month to accomplish your life's vision?
- How much do you need in assets?

- What do you need to have saved so that you can generate part of this income?
- What rate of return do you need on an annualized basis?

Understanding Risk

Understanding the rate of return that's needed to accomplish your life's vision is important, but what's even more critically important is knowing how much risk you're able to handle emotionally. In building a portfolio, this detail, if overlooked, can sabotage your success. If your financial plan says that you need to return north of 10 percent to realize your vision, you are going to have to take on a lot of risk. If you're not comfortable with risk or with seeing your portfolio fluctuate wildly, you will need to analyze your financial situation using a lower rate of return better suited to the amount of risk you are comfortable with. Remember, our objective is not to have to worry about money.

I always tell my clients that ensuring their comfort is indispensable to the financial plan. In fact, I believe it is the most important aspect of the entire financial planning process. As a financial professional, I must be diligent in understanding how much risk a client is willing to assume. If something happens in the economy and we experience a major downturn, that client may force me to sell out of their portfolio, which will be a major derailment and may well prevent realizing their long-term vision. From the start of the process, the risk conversation must be had and understood in detail. As an advisor, I know that I must get this right for each client's different needs.

Since 1926, the stock market has corrected greater than 10 percent numerous times. On occasion, the correction has been 20, 30, and even 40 percent or more. During the worst of all, the Great Depression, the stock market corrected 83 percent!

I don't believe that you need to over-analyze investing your capital. Instead, simply know and understand the past, present, and future risks. With my clients, I help them to assess risk and then decide what *feels* best for them specifically. One size does not fit all. With this settled, we go for that solution.

Of course, you will encounter several external risks, such as inflation, credit, industry/company, interest rates, the geopolitical situation, political and economic uncertainty, and currency and liquidity. All that you need to know and understand is that these things drive the stock market down, possibly to the percentages I have listed above. You can pontificate as much as you want in an effort to figure out how bad any one of these risks may get at any time but, in the end, pontification is just so much hot air. Instead, I focus with my clients on the big picture. We work to understand the facts, the risks, and what feels right for them. The best asset classes to invest in that will grow your wealth the most over time are stocks, private equity, and real estate. This is indisputable. If you're going to invest 100 percent of your money in these asset classes, then you will undoubtedly experience major downturns. The question you must ask yourself is this: *Can you emotionally handle the ups and downs associated with that risk?* If you have a 100 percent stock portfolio you will obtain the best performance *over time.*

Performance: Stocks, Bonds, Bills, and REITs
1972–2022

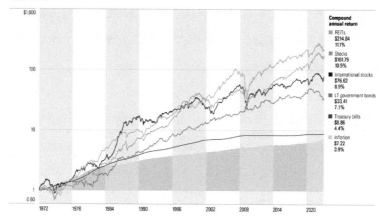

Past performance is no guarantee of future results. This is for illustrative purposes only and not indicative of any investment. An investment cannot be made directly in an index. © Morningstar 2023 and Precision Information, dba Financial Fitness Group 2023. All Rights Reserved. About the data: REITs are represented by the FTSE NAREIT All Equity REIT Index®, stocks by the Standard & Poor's 500®, which is an unmanaged group of securities and considered to be representative of the U.S. stock market in general, international stocks by the Morgan Stanley Capital International Europe, Australasia, and Far East (EAFE®) index, bonds by the 20-year U.S. government bond, and Treasury bills by the 30-day U.S. Treasury bill. Inflation is represented by the Consumer Price Index. An investment cannot be made directly in an index.

But you must fully understand that your portfolio can go through major downturns, which may last a long time. This being the case, you need to make sure—and I mean 100 percent sure—that you are comfortable with assuming that level of risk.

If you do not want to endure the gut-wrenching lows, your alternative is to build a well-balanced and diversified portfolio that can help to protect your capital during major downturns. By doing so, you will sacrifice some return. But as long as the return that you receive is sufficient to accomplish your life's vision, that's all you should care about. You should not focus on the investments of other family members or friends. It's not always about the latest and greatest, hyped-up investments that people throw money into. Often, these are overvalued and have a short lifespan. Nothing irritates me more than when a client calls to tell me how much money their friend is making in a certain risky part of the market and asks why we aren't investing in something like that. My answer is always the same: *We are not investing in those areas because you can't handle those risks, and you can accomplish your life's vision without taking on those types of uncertainties.*

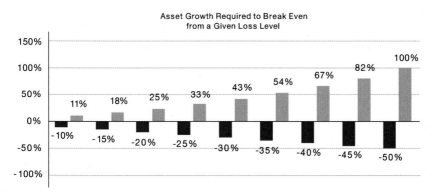

Asset Growth Required to Break Even from a Given Loss Level

PALUMBO
WEALTH MANAGEMENT
YOUR PERSONAL CFO

After I calmly repeat this to my clients, they always understand—eventually, anyway. Overall, you have to set the stage for yourself and not worry about what other people are doing. You don't know their full financial situation or the level of risk that they're taking on. All you have control over is your own financial situation, maintaining your life's vision, working out your own rate of return, what you personally need, and how much risk you're willing to take on. This should be your sole focus. Nothing else.

Avoiding risk is not all about self-denial. Understand that you *win* by minimizing your losses. If you are down 10 percent you need to return 11 percent to get yourself back to even. If you are down 50 percent, you need to be up 100 percent just to get back to even. Such a loss can eat up years to make up. If you are taking distributions for income purposes, this will only exacerbate the shortfall. I always discuss this with my clients and future clients because it's so important. When you have stopped working, you cannot afford to lose half your money for the obvious reason that you cannot go back and earn what took you twenty, thirty, or forty years to amass.

When I go through the financial planning process, I always review this scenario with my clients. It's important to see if it's possible to accomplish their vision while earning 3 percent on average over their lifetime. Now, I pretty much know I will outperform that. However, the point I'm making is that if I can take less risk to avoid major downturns and relieve some of the anxiety that clients typically feel, I always prefer to do that and so do my clients. To reiterate, the first part of building an investment strategy is understanding the rate of return that you need to accomplish your life's vision. Then ask yourself, based on history, if you can handle the ups and downs of the investment strategy you have chosen. Assuming that you're at a place where your risk tolerance has been analyzed in detail and it matches up with the rate of return that you are trying to achieve, your next step is to build certain philosophies and principles you feel sanguine about.

Building a Properly Balanced Portfolio

To be great at anything in life, you must do your homework and follow what the great people in your profession do. When it comes to portfolio construction, Ray Dalio is one of the best—maybe even *the* best. I have spent countless hours reading his books, reading about him, studying his research, and building my models around his philosophy. He is a true student of the markets, who spends time understanding the history of cause and effect and how it influences asset classes. You must look back at history and understand how certain asset classes perform in various economic environments. There are generally four economic environments you need to understand:

1. Economic growth is accelerating.
2. Economic growth is decelerating.
3. Inflation is accelerating.
4. Inflation is decelerating.

Two of these four economic environments may occur at any given time.

When economic growth accelerates, stocks and commodities can perform well. When economic growth decelerates, bonds and stocks can perform well. When inflation accelerates, commodities and gold tend to outperform stocks and bonds. When inflation decelerates, bonds perform very well.

I have researched these details going back to 1968, a time when gold traded freely on the market and, as of August 15, 1971, when President Richard Nixon "closed the gold window," so that the price of gold was no longer pegged to the dollar. The deep-dive analysis I performed helped me to understand these four economic environments and how specific asset classes performed historically in them. Today, however, I avoid speculating on which economic environment will prevail for the next twelve months. Why? Because such speculation is fruitless and such predictions are worthless. The environment's effects are never consistent. For example, if I felt that the economy was going to grow in the next twelve months, I would invest my client's capital 100 percent in stocks. The risk comes in if I am wrong about my forecast and economic growth decelerates. If that happens, my client's portfolio will suffer losses so severe that they may take years to recover.

I am accurate 70 percent of the time or more, but the one time that I am wrong can torpedo my client's long-term strategies and goals. This is precisely why, as a point of principle, I don't believe in "timing" the stock market, interest rates, or which direction the economy is headed.

Dangers of Market-Timing
Hypothetical Value of $1 Invested from 1926–2021

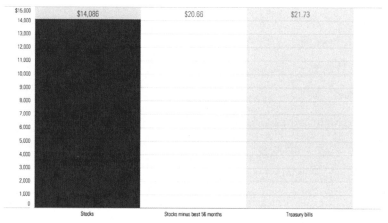

As you review the chart above, consider this example. If you were fully invested during 1926-2021, the span covered in the chart, your dollar grew to $14,086. If you missed the best fifty-six months (when the return averaged 4.9 percent) out of these 1,140 months, your dollar is now worth $20.66. This is a significant difference for someone who didn't remain in the market, versus an investor who stayed fully invested in the market for the entire time. Understanding this concept is imperative to comprehend how to properly balance a portfolio.

Balancing a Portfolio

The first step in understanding how to properly balance a portfolio is to make sure that you have exposure to the various economic environments I have outlined above. Investing your capital in stocks, treasury bonds, gold, and commodities is a good start toward building a more balanced portfolio. This is because when one asset class zigs, you want to be involved in another asset class that zags. If you have a portfolio that owns asset classes with identical correlations and those asset classes go down, they will go down in tandem, which is hardly the best way to protect your capital.

Correlations of Various Asset Classes with the Market
January 1980–December 2021

	Before recession Jan 1980–Dec 1999	During recession Jan 2000–Dec 2009	Post recession Jan 2010–Dec 2021
Small stocks	0.71	0.73	0.86
International stocks	0.51	0.88	0.87
Commodities	0.09	0.30	0.55
REITs	0.51	0.59	0.72
Gold	0.07	0.00	0.07
Long-term corporate bonds	0.33	0.12	-0.02
Long-term govt bonds	0.31	-0.14	-0.43
Intermediate-term govt bonds	0.26	-0.33	-0.37
Treasury bills	-0.09	-0.04	-0.11

■ High
■ Medium
■ Low

When you invest in non-correlated asset classes, the benefit is added balance. If there's a collapse in the stock market or economy, you then have built-in asset classes that will protect your capital. That is the benefit. The negative side is that you will sacrifice some upside return to gain some protection against an economic collapse. Look at the example of two uncorrelated asset classes based on the chart.

In the various correlations during different time periods, versus the S&P 500, you can see that during recession periods long-term government bonds and the S&P 500 are negatively correlated. Gold has a zero correlation with stocks and commodities, which ultimately adds diversification benefits. This means that you are properly balancing your portfolio.

An important part of investing your capital is understanding that your asset allocation essentially drives the performance that you will achieve—but also the risk. Asset allocation is even more important than stock selection and market timing. There are many studies, including one done by IBM many years ago, that asset allocation accounts for more than 90 percent of the risk-adjusted return you receive from the money that you invest. For this reason alone, it is imperative that you focus on understanding how to properly balance your portfolio. Ultimately, this is going to be the return and the risk that you will endure for the rest of your life.

In What Investment Vehicles Should You Invest?

Once the concept of balancing your portfolio is understood, you must decide what investment vehicles to use within the confines of your balanced portfolio. Through my own research and experience, I think low-cost investment vehicles are the way to go. I have always personally used single stocks with no underlying expenses, single bonds with no underlying expenses, and exchange-traded funds that have very low underlying expenses. Research proves that mutual funds and actively managed strategies with higher underlying expenses and/ or commissions tend to underperform the general market. That's a problem. If you are paying a mutual fund money manager or a separately managed account manager, you need your investments to be managed to outperform their indexes. The fact is you are usually better off owning the general S&P 500 market through an exchange-traded fund at a much lower expense ratio. You must be very careful when looking at what investment vehicles you use to build your portfolio.

I have always liked to invest in a combination of single stocks, single bonds, and ETFs because of the low-cost construction. They are also very easy to trade. On single stocks, if you want to be great at identifying stocks of wonderful businesses, you should study the countless books, articles, and videos about Warren Buffett's philosophy. He and Charlie Munger are the greatest of all time, so putting the work to research these men will be a game-changer for you. Understand above all that you don't need to own fifty, sixty, a hundred, or two hundred stocks to be diversified. You can own twenty to thirty in different sectors and be amply diversified. The key is to make sure you do your homework and understand all the different stocks of businesses that you're going to own.

Here are my 13 fundamental principles of investing in stocks of great businesses that I believe will help you be successful:

1. Strong free cash flow yield (see below) that is more than the ten-year risk-free treasury yield.

2. High return on invested capital of at least 15%.

3. Predictable business model with stable earnings over a ten-year period.

4. Durable competitive advantage or wide economic "moat".

5. Sell products or services that you are using yourself, or people around you are using.

6. Simple businesses that you truly understand and have a slow rate of change.

7. Great leadership with a proven track record.

8. Earnings that are growing faster than the S&P 500. Charlie Munger said, "He would rather own a great company at a fair price, then a fair company at a great price".

9. Use a margin of safety in the event your calculations are incorrect. More specifically, buy businesses that are trading at a discount of at least 30% to its intrinsic value. Learn how to discount future cash flows to arrive at the intrinsic value of a business.

10. Be patient. Give the business at a minimum three years to converge to your intrinsic value estimate.

11. Study what other successful investors are purchasing.

12. Stop saying you own a stock and watching it trade on a daily basis. YOU ARE WASTING YOUR TIME! You own a slice of a business and you are a long-term investor. If you did your due diligence properly, your business will realize its intrinsic value over time. Benjamin Graham, Warren Buffett's mentor, said, "In the short-term, the stock market is a voting machine, but in the long-term, it is a weighing machine."

13. Stop trying to figure out the macro environment and timing the market. Time and time again, we know this is a complete waste of time. When Mr. Market gives you an opportunity to invest in a great business that is trading cheap because of a macro economic situation, then take advantage of that. Don't run from it!

Free cash flow (FCF) is the cash a company generates after accounting for outlays to support operations and maintain its capital assets. Unlike earnings or net income, FCF excludes the non-cash expenses reported on the company's income statement but includes expenditures on equipment and assets as well as changes in the company's working capital. FCF is calculated by taking the net income of a company, adding back depreciation and amortization, and subtracting capital expenditures. You then take that figure and divide it by the market cap of where the company is trading in the public markets on that particular day. Because FCF is a highly accurate measure of profitability, you should obsess about the FCF yield of an investment you are contemplating and compare it to the ten-year treasury yield, an investment considered risk-free. For example, when Warren Buffett started investing in Apple Stock in the first quarter of 2016, Apple stock had a free cash flow yield of approximately 10 percent plus. The ten-year risk-free rate was at that time yielding 2.4 percent. The way Warren Buffett looked at Apple was that they were producing a free cash flow yield that was almost 4.5 times what the risk-free rate was yielding.

Apple also had what Buffett famously calls a "wide moat." A moat is a competitive advantage that gives a business the ability to overperform with outsized profits. Apple's moat? Hey, guess what? Everyone has an iPhone!

Since Buffett's first purchase, his company's investment in Apple is up 546 percent versus the S&P 500, which is up 124 percent from March 31, 2016 to July 29, 2022. If you learn anything from this book, please learn to *obsess about* the free cash flow yield of an investment relative to the ten-year treasury's risk-free rate of return.

We consider the ten-year treasury *the* risk-free rate of return because there is a high probability that the United States government will not go bankrupt and will therefore be able to pay you your interest and return your principal after ten years. There is so much uncertainty around how a company is going to grow and succeed over a ten-year period that when it comes to investing in stocks (or real estate or any other risky investment), you want to make sure you are getting paid for the risk. Seeking two to four times the ten-year treasury yield is a great rule of thumb. Adhering to the key principles in this and the paragraph above will make a tremendous difference in your investment success over your lifetime.

The final principle I want to share with you comes from the Peter Lynch approach, which is important for becoming a long-term investor. When you own predictable businesses that have been around for a long time and have strong free cash flow, you enjoy an element of protection that gives comfort to investors. The opposite would be owning stocks of businesses that are growing rapidly but have no earnings and are borrowing a lot of money to fuel the enterprise. My concern with these types of businesses is that, due to their high debt and no earnings, they get hurt badly when an economic downturn comes along. Additionally, such stocks can go down rapidly in a short period of time. I have always believed that the stock market is essentially volatile and highly unpredictable. When you include stocks that are speculative, you compound the inherent unpredictability with even more unpredictability. This is why I feel much more comfortable owning stocks of great businesses that my clients know and understand. From my experience, when downturns occur, having a strong foundation gives you a margin of comfort.

On the bonds side, I prefer to own individual bonds that encompass defined maturities and blend in treasury ETFs. This can act as a buffer when stocks go down. Owning individual bonds with defined maturities offers my clients predictability, no matter how their principal may fluctuate due to interest rates. As interest rates rise, your principal invested in bonds will decline, and vice versa. If you purchase a bond for par $100 and interest rates then rise, your statement could report the value of your bond as $95. If your bond matures in three years, you will receive $100. From a psychological standpoint, clients feel comfortable in that kind of predictability.

In gold and commodities, I also use exchange-traded funds. With these, it is imperative that you do your research to make sure that there is adequate volume per day, the expense ratios are all reasonable relative to their competitors, and you fully understand how a particular ETF trades gold and commodities. Always make certain to compare one commodity ETF versus the others before you invest. If you have two ETFs with the exact same performance and underlying strategy but one has a higher expense ratio than the other, invest in the lower-cost option. Do your homework to understand the differences.

Finally, never, never, never forget the importance of having a written financial plan. Think of it as the guide that you will use for the rest of your life to maximize the wealth for which you have worked so hard. A good financial plan will stress-test your situation to make sure that you have no risk of running out of money. Once the stress test has been passed, you will need to work to fully understand the various risks of investing your capital and what you're most comfortable with. Finally, work to build a properly balanced portfolio that can withstand economic downturns while maintaining performance.

CHAPTER 9

SURVIVING DURING AN ECONOMIC IMPLOSION

Everything I share with you in this book has been written to help you to avoid significant mistakes that could drive you off course in your journey toward a work-optional life. But it's not all on you. Economics and economies are complex and far from perfectly predictable. One of the most challenging tasks for a financial planner is coaching clients through the economic hiccups and outright implosions that will almost certainly occur throughout your life.

Both the planning professional and the client need to understand the emotional dimension of these situations. How you react to the stress that comes with experiencing risks must factor into whatever investment strategy you and your advisor create. Too many wealth managers minimize the emotional aspect of investing. Not me. I remind them that a big part of our purpose is to stop worrying about their money. Emotion looms large in investment, and it should!

Knowledge and understanding are critical to managing emotion effectively. The greatest source of fear is the unknown. So, another thing I tell my clients is that before they invest their money it is important to fully understand the history of the various markets. Now, some of the information that I'm going to share in this chapter may feel a bit redundant. If so, please indulge me. I repeat only what is most important for you to know, anticipate, and understand. Believe me, the more you know, the less you will worry.

Economic Downturns

The past hundred years or more have seen long-term bull markets in which the Dow Jones Industrial Average (DJI) returned anywhere from 8 to 24 percent per year over six to twenty-four-year stretches. But there have also been long-term bear markets, in which the DJI was flat to negative over a long period. An example of historical research is a chart by Ned Davis, covering the twenty-five-year period from 1942 to 1966.

During this span, the Dow Jones averaged 10.5 percent returns before inflation per year. During the so-called Roaring Twenties, 1921 to 1929, the DJI average was around 24.9 percent per year. Prior to this extended boom, the Dow index saw the opposite. From 1906 to 1921, the Dow averaged -1.1 percent. From 1966 to 1982, the DJI performed even more poorly, losing -1.5 percent per year.

Why review so much history? Well, we are all living in what will someday be history. That's reality. And if you have 100 percent of your money in stocks and are working within a long-term bear market, you may end up derailing the execution of your financial plan. Understand that you will never know if you are entering into either a long-term bull or a long-term bear market. This is why I advocate having a well-balanced portfolio capable of performing well no matter the economic environment in which the world finds itself. During the long-term bear market of 1966 to 1982, gold and commodities performed well and were effective diversifiers that were helpful in creating a balanced portfolio.

History of Investments

Market Downturns and Recoveries
1926–2022

Downturn	% Loss			Recovery
34 months	83.4	Sep 1929 – June 1932	July 1932 – Jan 1945	151 months
6 months	-21.8	June 1946 – Nov 1946	Dec 1946 – Oct 1949	35 months
7 months	-10.2	Aug 1956 – Feb 1957	Mar 1957 – July 1957	5 months
5 months	-15.0	Aug 1957 – Dec 1957	Jan 1958 – July 1958	7 months
6 months	-22.3	Jan 1962 – June 1962	July 1962 – Apr 1963	10 months
8 months	-15.6	Feb 1966 – Sep 1966	Oct 1966 – Mar 1967	6 months
19 months	-29.3	Dec 1968 – June 1970	July 1970 – Mar 1971	9 months
21 months	-42.6	Jan 1973 – Sep 1974	Oct 1974 – June 1976	21 months
14 months	-14.3	Jan 1977 – Feb 1978	Mar 1978 – July 1978	5 months
20 months	-16.5	Dec 1980 – July 1982	Aug 1982 – Oct 1982	3 months
3 months	-29.6	Sep 1987 – Nov 1987	Dec 1987 – May 1989	18 months
5 months	-14.7	June 1990 – Oct 1990	Nov 1990 – Feb 1991	4 months
2 months	-15.4	July 1998 – Aug 1998	Sep 1998 – Nov 1998	3 months
25 months	-44.7	Sep 2000 – Sep 2002	Oct 2002 – Oct 2006	49 months
16 months	-50.9	Nov 2007 – Feb 2009	Mar 2009 – Mar 2012	37 months
3 months	13.5	Oct 2018 – Dec 2018	Jan 2019 – Apr 2019	4 months
3 months	-19.6	Dec 2019 – Mar 2020	Apr 2020 – June 2020	3 months
10 months	-23.9	Dec 2021 – Sep 2022		

PALUMBO
WEALTH MANAGEMENT
YOUR PERSONAL CFO

While it may be more fun to look back at bull markets, it is more important to examine the history of the major bear market downturns for help in building a balanced portfolio. Look into periods during which large US company stocks took long downward turns. During the Great Depression, which started in 1929, large US company stocks went down a staggering -83.4 percent from peak to trough.

Or look at the three-year period between 2000 and 2002, which included the collapse of the dot-com tech bubble and the 9/11 terrorist attacks. US large-company stocks declined -44.7%. During the so-called Great Recession, from November 2007 to February 2009, the stock market was down -50.9%.

I share this with you because, first, *it happened* and, second, it is important to understand all the factors and risks when you are building a balanced portfolio. History provides ample proof of large stock market drawdowns. They are not rare, and, often, they are not short-term. This should motivate you to ask yourself—honestly—if you are comfortable with a significant percentage of your money being exposed to stocks. The lesson of history here is that the stock market is prone to steep and protracted declines as well as gains. The risk of a large downturn or downturns is considerable during your lifetime. The time to think about this is before you make your financial plan. Stocks are a reasonable option as part of a plan, but you must truly understand and accept the real risk of living through a downturn. As you begin to plan, listen to what your feelings tell you about your tolerance for risk. Remember, you do not want to worry about your money. Balance this goal against your desire for high returns. Determine how much money you need to become work-optional by a specified time. Do not push your risk beyond the point at which your investment plan is highly likely to attain your goal. You must prepare yourself emotionally for all the consequences and results your plan may have. This helps you to succeed without making a panic-driven emotional mistake.

Periods of Consecutive Negative Stock Returns
1926–2021

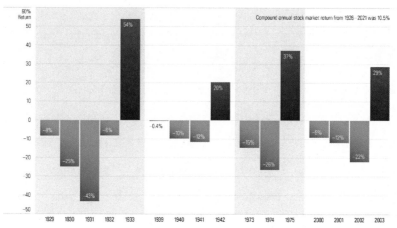

Another point to bear in mind is that, as important as your emotional well-being is, you do not have to become a helpless victim of economic factors beyond your control. Your financial plan should include potential strategies for retaining money and even, in effect, getting "lost years" back after large-company stocks experience a downturn.

If you look at the data from 1926 to 2021, you will see multiple rebounds, which created bull markets. You may also note that these do not occur as often as you might think they would. In the long run, during the period from 1926 to 2021—which saw the Great Depression and other lesser but still major recessions—the compound annual return from stocks was 10.5 percent. But how long can you hold your breath in the troughs? Let me repeat my advice: plan as conservatively as possible consistently to reach your goals.

With respect to the history of investments, I have another idea to share with you. It is the concept of investing new money during recessions, or "rebalancing your portfolio." This means selling the asset classes that go up when stocks go down or buying stocks that are down. Either of these strategies or a combination of the two may yield the best performance over time when applied during a recession.

An example of this can be seen in the chart.

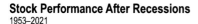

Stock Performance After Recessions
1953–2021

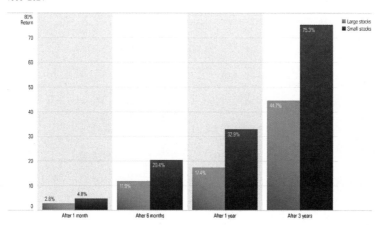

Past performance is no guarantee of future results. Cumulative returns of large and small stocks after recessions 1953–2021. This is for illustrative purposes only and not indicative of any investment. An investment cannot be made directly in an index. © Morningstar 2022 and Precision Information, dba Financial Fitness Group 2022. All Rights Reserved.

If you had put your money to work at the end of every recession starting in 1953, you'd have a return of 17.4 percent for large-company stocks and 32.9 percent for small caps after one year. After three years, large-company stocks would be up 44.7 percent and small-cap stocks would rise to 75.3 percent. This illustrates the principle of putting new capital to work during the end of recessions and/or rebalancing your portfolio to take advantage of stocks going down.

Something else to consider during recessionary periods is that many investors totally surrender their rational selves to emotion. At these times, my clients often want to sell their stocks and "wait it out," planning to get back in whenever the outlook improves. I tell them that getting out when you go through difficult times is not the major issue. To get a successful return, you must *get back in* at just the right moment. This means that your odds are down because you need to predict correctly twice, getting out and getting in. In fact, this is a nearly impossible feat. Even more important, when clients who are business owners or own real estate ask me to sell their stocks, I respond by asking them if they plan to sell their business or real estate. "Of course not," they answer—because they understand that, in a recession, those values fall, which means they will lose money if they sell.

"If your answer is no, you're not selling your real estate," I ask, "then why are you selling your stocks in these great businesses?" The point I am making to them is that you should look at your investment in the stocks of great businesses no differently from how you look at your own business or your real estate holdings. All are long-term, free cash-flow-generating investments, and your short-term, emotion-driven view of the economy or markets should not deter you from your long-term investment discipline. If successful real estate investors had the ability to sell their real estate in an open public market like stocks, do you think they would have had as much success? Absolutely not. When you make an investment in a stock of a wonderful business, you should pretend you cannot sell it for at least ten years.

The following chart shows data from the Great Recession of 2007 to 2009.

The Importance of Staying Invested
Ending Wealth Values After a Market Decline

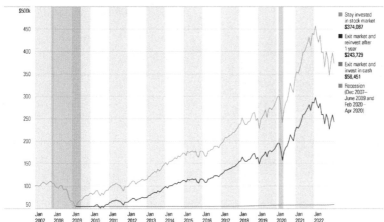

As an investor, if you stayed fully in throughout that period—up until the end of 2021—rather than exiting the market and reinvesting later on, you would have been much better off. This is precisely why I advocate against trying to time the stock market. I know I just discussed this, but I want to hammer home market timing. Look at the chart. Had you stayed fully invested in all 5.036 trading days from 2002 through 2021, your return would have been 9.5%. If you missed the 10 best days, your return was cut by more than 50% to 5.3%. If you missed the best 50 days, your return was negative. This is a great illustration of just how risky it is to time-out the market. This data tells you unequivocally that when you get it wrong, you will fully or partly derail your financial plan.

If you take away a single message from this chapter, make it this: Be a long-term investor. Completely selling out of stocks because you anticipate an economic downturn is a losing game. Look at this chart, and you will see that during major stock market declines—after one year, three years, and five years—markets recover and often come back stronger.

The Cost of Market-Timing
The Risk of Missing the Best Days in the Market, 2003-2022

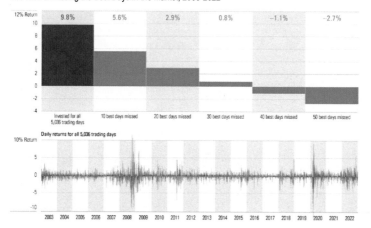

U.S. Market Recovery After Financial Crises
Cumulative Return of All-Stock Portfolio After Various Events

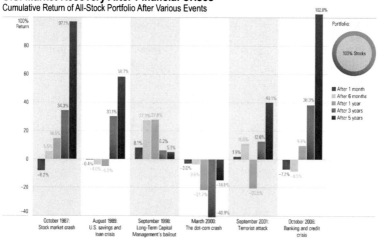

This is what the data tell us. Nevertheless, if you are a long-term investor, you should avoid owning 100% stocks. If you are caught in a long-term bear market, your returns may be negative over a long period. That is why properly balancing your portfolio with non-correlated asset classes and then rebalancing when there is a dislocation with one or two of the asset classes, is the winning strategy.

CHAPTER 10

MY WEALTH MANAGEMENT FORMULA

One thing years of experience in this industry have taught me is that most folks don't know what wealth management is. Ask ten people picked at random what they think wealth management means, and you'll get ten different answers. Even worse, ten wealth managers will give you another ten. Now, I hope the first eight chapters of this book have brought some enlightenment, but, as a public service, I have also created a formula to keep you out of the weeds by streamlining the definition of wealth management. Here it is:

$$WM=IC+AP+RM$$

"WM" is *wealth management.*

"IC" is *investment consultant,* which refers to how you should invest your money based on everything that we have discussed in the prior chapters. A wealth manager (a professional like me) can be your consultant and can also direct you to other financial specialists who can provide additional expertise in specialized areas of managing and investing your assets. But you should consider this book as your first IC.

Let's pause here to note that, before you invest, you must understand the vision that you have for your life now and for the rest of it, what your lifestyle costs will be, and the income sources needed to pay for that lifestyle. Next, you must run through a detailed financial analysis to confirm that you can in fact achieve your life's vision. Once you accomplish that goal, it's time to invest based on your own personal financial plan. This is the only way to ensure that you can and will accomplish your life's vision. We have covered some of these processes already, but review them now, as a checklist: Define your life's vision.

1. Determine the cost of realizing the lifestyle part of this vision
2. Save assets and know what you have.
3. Look into various income sources.
4. Work with a detailed analysis of your finances to confirm that you can achieve your vision.
5. Know how much risk you are comfortable taking as an investor.
6. Settle on a rational design for managing your portfolio.
7. Know when and how to rebalance your portfolio as necessary.

Going Deeper

Now, I've taken you only as far as the "WM" and the "IC." This will lead you toward solving the first part of my formula. But we need to go to the AP portion, "Advanced Planning." Here is where you must get very organized about your finances.

You need to gather all the documents relating to your taxes, estate and trust, property and casualty coverage, life insurance, long-term care insurance, asset protection coverages, charitable giving, and family governance. For AP, the first call to action, then, is to gather all these documents and organize them in a single location. Ideally, digitize everything, so that it can be encrypted and sent to specialized consultants through an online portal.

Once you have organized your documents, you should be able to detect any gaps or situations that leave you exposed and need to be addressed quickly. To proceed with the next step, the "RM"—Relationship Management—part of the formula, you need to review your documents with a professional who specializes in each of the areas I mentioned in the preceding paragraph. For example, to fully understand your tax situation, you should have your last two years of tax returns reviewed by a CPA, who can assist you in making sure you are doing all you can to minimize taxes—not just today, on a single return, but in the long term, as taxes relate to your future vision for your life.

Investing your money properly by managing risk is an important part of your overall financial plan but minimizing taxes throughout your journey can be even more important. In addition to securing an outside CPA to review your taxes, you can also consider specialists in the categories of estate and trust planning, insurance—life, property, casualty, charitable giving, and, if you are a business owner, business insurance. There are professionals available for consultation in all these important areas of your finances. They can review your documents and make certain you have not overlooked anything important. I have much more to say about minimizing your taxes in Chapter 12.

I will never forget the time I took on a new client who had an estate tax problem. I had to persuade him—maybe "push" is the more accurate word—to go see an estate planning attorney, so that he could review the gaps that I had noticed in his plan while reviewing his overall financial plan. Following his review, the estate planner suggested that my client set up certain trusts to mitigate federal and state estate taxes. My client balked at the attorney's proposed fee for designing his estate plan.

"Phil!" he gasped as soon as I picked up his call. "There's no way I'm paying this! Can you call the attorney to try to reduce the cost?"

The proposed fee was $8,000, which I was able to negotiate down to $6,000. My client agreed to proceed. Six months later, he passed away. With the help of the attorney's plan, I was able to save his family $400,000 in state estate taxes. That amount was added to their wealth, and it was a large sum for them to retain.

The point of this example is that you absolutely need a written financial plan that covers more than just your investments, going deeper to cover advanced planning. The effort and expense of bringing in relevant experts can pay off in maximizing personal wealth throughout your lifetime and beyond, benefitting the loved ones who live on after you.

I know that putting work and cash into the creation of a full financial plan can seem like a daunting process. And it does indeed take work to gather all the necessary information, organize it, and then review all of it, piece by piece, with possibly more than one outside professional. After more than two decades as a wealth advisor, however, I can promise you that the reward is well worth the time, expense, and discipline needed to drive you forward in creating and executing a great plan.

Look at it this way. Once you have everything in a central location—organized in a binder *and* encrypted online—you will have access to all the records of your financial life anytime you need it. This alone should increase your level of comfort with your financial situation. It will also facilitate any additional planning or adjustments you need or want to make for years to come. Whether it's looking at your marginal tax rate in prior years or learning what it will be in the coming year, all you need to do is flip to the tab in your binder or go online for immediate access to all the answers to all your questions. With your information organized and available at your fingertips, you are equipped with the knowledge and wisdom you need to cope with changing times and circumstances. This is key to the core of my purpose, which is, first and foremost, helping my clients achieve peace of mind when it comes to their personal finances. Knowledge is power, and this kind of power brings you confidence and peace.

CHAPTER 11

YOUR LIFE, YOUR HEALTHCARE

Let's return now to the first leg of our three-legged stool of life: your personal health. If you do not look after your health, you can't care properly for your family (leg 2), and the money (leg 3) that you worked so hard to earn is put in peril. The lives and welfare of you and your family need all three legs of the stool. Health, family, and money are all interdependent, and each is indispensable. True, if you are not smart with your money, you will never be able to enjoy all the amazing things life has to offer, but you cannot let yourself be driven exclusively by money. You may have the good fortune to be a multimillionaire or billionaire, but unless you have health and a loving family, your wealth is of little use to you.

Earlier, I discussed the importance of balancing and, when necessary, rebalancing your portfolio. Heed the words of Denzel Washington when he says, "At your highest moment, be careful. That's when the devil comes for you." As you must balance your portfolio properly, you must also balance your life, ensuring that the three legs on which it rests are all looked after and kept strong. These are your pillars of true success and happiness.

Healthcare Costs

Let's drill down on healthcare. As you unlock a work-optional lifestyle, healthcare costs are an important factor in your financial planning, especially before you qualify for Medicare coverage at age sixty-five. The chart demonstrates what you likely already know: healthcare costs represent a large percentage of our annual spending; moreover, inflation is the highest in this area.

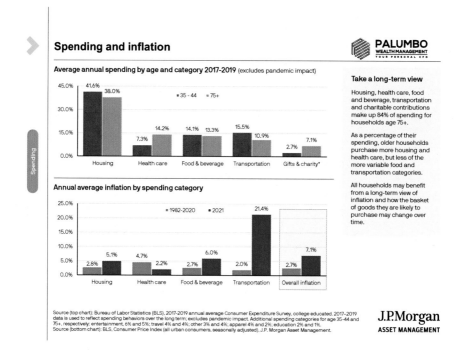

The estimated monthly health insurance cost for individuals under sixty-five years old can be as low as $641 a month or as high as $1,634 per month, depending on the plan you select and your health condition.

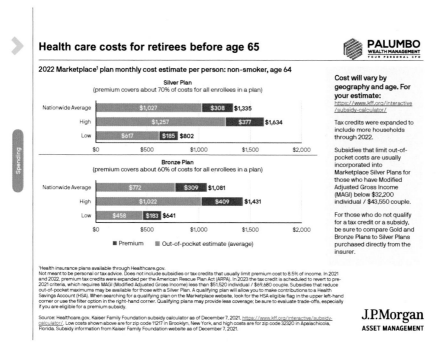

Important components of healthcare costs include more than your monthly insurance premium. You need to look at your plan's deductibles, co-pays, and prescription costs. You also need to adjust your calculations if your spouse works and has a healthcare plan that covers you as well.

If you are sixty-five or older, you are eligible to enroll in Medicare and purchase a supplemental plan as well, which will defray the portion of your healthcare expenses Medicare alone does not cover. Medicare Part A covers inpatient hospital care and is free. Part B covers doctor visits, tests, and outpatient hospital visits. Part B monthly costs vary, based on the average of your income over the past two years. Part D is a relatively new addition to Medicare and covers prescriptions. (There is a Part C, "Medicare Advantage," which is an alternate way of getting Medicare benefits that applies to a minority of Medicare recipients.)

The chart shows the combined cost of Parts B and D as of 2022, based on your modified adjusted gross income.

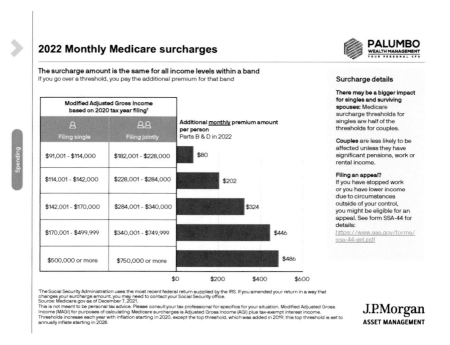

2022 Monthly Medicare surcharges

The surcharge amount is the same for all income levels within a band
If you go over a threshold, you pay the additional premium for that band

Modified Adjusted Gross Income based on 2020 tax year filing¹		Additional *monthly* premium amount per person Parts B & D in 2022
Filing single	Filing jointly	
$91,001 - $114,000	$182,001 - $228,000	$80
$114,001 - $142,000	$228,001 - $284,000	$202
$142,001 - $170,000	$284,001 - $340,000	$324
$170,001 - $499,999	$340,001 - $749,999	$446
$500,000 or more	$750,000 or more	$486

$0 $200 $400 $600

¹The Social Security Administration uses the most recent federal return supplied by the IRS. If you amended your return in a way that changes your surcharge amount, you may need to contact your Social Security office.
Source: Medicare.gov as of December 7, 2021.
This is not meant to be personal tax advice. Please consult your tax professional for specifics for your situation. Modified Adjusted Gross Income (MAGI) for purposes of calculating Medicare surcharges is Adjusted Gross Income (AGI) plus tax-exempt interest income. Thresholds increase each year with inflation starting in 2020, except the top threshold, which was added in 2019; this top threshold is set to annually inflate starting in 2028.

Surcharge details

There may be a bigger impact for singles and surviving spouses: Medicare surcharge thresholds for singles are half of the thresholds for couples.

Couples are less likely to be affected unless they have significant pensions, work or rental income.

Filing an appeal?
If you have stopped work or you have lower income due to circumstances outside of your control, you might be eligible for an appeal. See form SSA-44 for details:
https://www.ssa.gov/forms/ssa-44-ext.pdf

If you are married and filing jointly with a modified adjusted gross income of $400,000, your combined cost for Medicare Part B and Part D is $446 a month.

Finally, you might add a Medigap supplemental insurance policy and a vision, dental, and hearing plan because Parts A and B may not have all the coverage you want. This comes at another additional cost per month. Look at the chart, for a breakdown of the costs of the healthcare options you should be thinking about. The chart also shows the rising costs of healthcare over time.

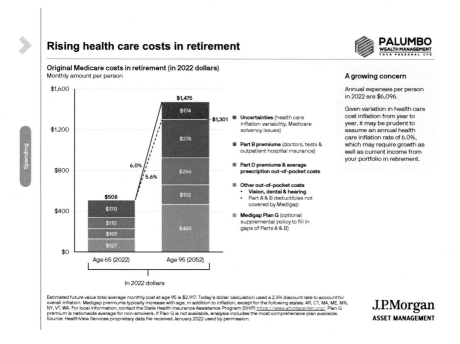

Rising health care costs in retirement

PALUMBO
WEALTH MANAGEMENT
YOUR PERSONAL CFO

Original Medicare costs in retirement (in 2022 dollars)
Monthly amount per person

A growing concern

Annual expenses per person in 2022 are $6,096.

Given variation in health care cost inflation from year to year, it may be prudent to assume an annual health care inflation rate of 6.0%, which may require growth as well as current income from your portfolio in retirement.

Age 65 (2022): $508 total — $170, $110, $101, $127
6.0% / 5.6%
Age 95 (2052): $1,301 / $1,475 total — $174, $378, $266, $192, $465

$1,600 / $1,200 / $800 / $400 / $0

Spending

- **Uncertainties** (health care inflation variability, Medicare solvency issues)
- **Part B premiums** (doctors, tests & outpatient hospital insurance)
- **Part D premiums & average prescription out-of-pocket costs**
- **Other out-of-pocket costs**
  - Vision, dental & hearing
  - Part A & B deductibles not covered by Medigap
- **Medigap Plan G** (optional supplemental policy to fill in gaps of Parts A & B)

In 2022 dollars

Estimated future value total average monthly cost at age 95 is $2,917. Today's dollar calculation used a 2.3% discount rate to account for overall inflation. Medigap premiums typically increase with age, in addition to inflation, except for the following states: AR, CT, MA, ME, MN, NY, VT, WA. For local information, contact the State Health Insurance Assistance Program (SHIP) https://www.shiptacenter.org/. Plan G premium is nationwide average for non-smokers. If Plan G is not available, analysis includes the most comprehensive plan available.
Source: HealthView Services proprietary data file received January 2022 used by permission.

J.P.Morgan
ASSET MANAGEMENT

Healthcare is both crucial and complicated. You need to do your homework so that you understand your potential and likely costs, including your potential worst-case scenario costs. Major health crises such as open-heart surgery or surgical and other cancer treatments can be life-altering and may come with monetary costs that are also capable of changing your life. Study your coverages and out-of-pocket expenses. The objective is to minimize surprises.

Long-Term Care

None of my clients enjoys paying premiums for something that they may never use, whether it's automobile insurance, homeowners insurance, and every other form of insurance we pay in the hope that we will never use it. But there is a new reality in healthcare. It is a consequence of the great advances in medicine and drugs that have enabled people to live longer today than ever before. Yet even as our bodies live longer, our minds continue aging and tend to become vulnerable to the likes of dementia and Alzheimer's Disease. Diseases such as these—and others—typically require long-term care, which family members are often unable to administer. This is a real issue, and there is an abundance of statistics floating around on the probability of each of us needing care at a long-term facility.

The thing is, statistics are not synonymous with truth. The insurance industry is highly motivated to market long-term care insurance. Some statistics emanating from that industry claim a 70 percent chance of your ending your years in a long-term care facility. As the chart shows, it is true that each of us has a 64 to 75 percent chance of requiring some form of long-term care.

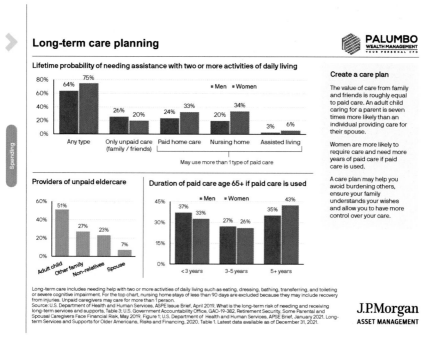

But this figure includes family or friends providing support for you, paid in-home care, moving into a nursing home, or moving into an assisted living facility. It is more accurate to point out that the lifetime probability of needing to go to a nursing home ranges from 20 to 34 percent for both males and females. In the case of a married couple, at least one spouse is likely going to require some form of long-term care, but the other spouse may be able to provide care in the home, with or without some professional assistance. This would certainly reduce costs, and that would be a good thing since the national annual median for a private room in a nursing home is about $105,850 per year (J.P. Morgan). The average range is anywhere from $85,200 to $135,000 per year, depending on where you live. If you are fifty-five years old today and you inflate these numbers up to when you'll be eighty-five, this could potentially cost $500,000 to $1 million or even more to fund, depending on the duration of your care. About a third to half of all human beings need paid care—but only for two years or less. The other 50 percent end up needing a long-term care in a paid facility for greater than two years. Most people decide to purchase long-term care insurance to cover the cost of extended care with the objective of ensuring that more money goes to the family when the person under care dies.

Any way you look at it, the need for long-term care is real. What the mix will be between care in a live-in facility and home care with and without professional assistance is open to question. Here are some options for funding, but in the end, you must decide what is best for you.

1. **Self-fund:** This means that you save enough money to pay for care without insurance. If your total net worth is $10 million, and you need only $5 million to enjoy life, the balance can be set aside to fund any type of long-term care you may need in the future. Some people are capable of this and comfortable with it. If you are not, keep reading.

2. **Traditional long-term care insurance:** You can purchase traditional long-term care insurance and pay monthly premiums until you either need care or die. With this type of product, the issue is that the premiums can rise. If you end up never needing care, you and others may feel like they have wasted money. But all insurance is a hedge against risk that may never come to pass. Long-term care insurance buys long-term care, if and when needed. But your payments are not really wasted if the insurance is never needed. The insurance buys you and others valuable peace of mind for many, many years.

3. **Life insurance with a long-term care rider:** With this model, you will pay monthly premiums. If you need paid long-term care assistance, this product will fund your care. If you never need care, your family will get a death benefit. Some people like this option, because they feel that, one way or another, their premiums will go toward some realized benefit. The cost of this option, however, is generally higher than the cost of traditional long-term care insurance.

4. **Hybrid long-term care insurance:** This is a one-time (large) upfront cost that will give your family a certain level of benefit and long-term care coverage. Some people like this

option, because they're able to fund this policy with $150,000 to $200,000, and the family may get that money back when the person dies. If the person ends up needing long-term care assistance, this type of policy can be of value.

5. **Medicaid asset protection trust:** In this situation, you would move most of your assets and retitle them into a new trust. If you need care more than five years from the date that you set up this trust, you can apply for Medicaid, and the state cannot come after your money. If you need care less than five years after, the money in the trust will be used to fund your care. Often, clients will do this when they're younger versus waiting until the last minute. Throughout my career, I've received positive feedback on this strategy. Clients like not having to pay for long-term care premiums and their assets are protected after five years of establishing and funding the trust with their assets. What people don't like about this option, however, is relinquishing control because this trust is irrevocable. It is important to understand this and be certain the option makes sense for you.

These are the core options to review for protecting your estate from the potential cost of long-term care. The message I want to convey loud and clear is, at a bare minimum, to have a plan. Review these detailed options and choose the one you are most comfortable with. Make sure your family is aware of the strategy you choose before you actually need long-term care.

CHAPTER 12

YOUR WORK-OPTIONAL LEGACY

I f you've come this far in my book, I probably don't have to sell you on the concept of making work optional in your life. But being able to walk away from your job is not the whole work-optional story. Let's discuss what it means to create a *work-optional legacy*.

We need to begin by talking about the last step in creating a financial plan that will position you for making work optional: dividing your money into three different buckets.

Dividing Your Money

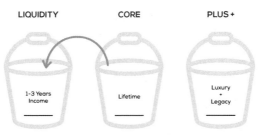

The first bucket is for your LIQUIDITY money. Bucket number two is for your CORE money. Bucket three will hold your PLUS money. Your planning task is to figure out how much money is needed to fill (fund) each bucket.

A great first step in this process is to go back to your financial-planning tools and try to reduce the amount of money that you are inputting by $250,000 increments. Here's what I mean by that. Let's say you spend $100,000 per year and have a total of $4 million in liquid money, including both non-retirement and retirement assets. In your financial planning tool, you would include $3,750,000 rather than $4,000,000. Then, you would run a full analysis to see if you can live a work-optional lifestyle on that amount of money. If the answer is yes, then reduce it by another $250,000. Keep reducing until you understand just how much of the $4 million you will actually need to live the lifestyle that you envision. If that number is $3.5 million, you know that $500,000 of your $4 million will not be needed to maintain your current lifestyle for the rest of your life, assuming you live to ninety-five. With this reduction step, we aid your financial planning by drilling down to your very personalized situation.

The next step in the process is to set up your three buckets. Continuing with our example, you fund your LIQUIDITY bucket with enough money to cover your cost of living for twelve full months or two or three years, depending on how conservative you want to be. A conservative approach is to fund your liquidity bucket with three years' worth of expenses, factoring in inflation. The person who does this need not worry about dipping into their CORE bucket for three years, an approach that increases peace of mind. The downside, however, is that the money invested in the LIQUIDITY bucket for three years earns a low rate of return since liquid investments necessarily generate less interest than longer-term investments. Your decision, then, depends on what you are most comfortable with. Let's assume you need $160,000 per year for lifestyle costs and you decide to fund it for only one year. Your first bucket, your LIQUIDITY bucket, will therefore be funded with $160,000, covering your lifestyle costs for twelve months. The difference of $3,500,000 minus $160,000, which is $3,340,000, will fund bucket two, the CORE bucket. These two buckets will be used to cover the costs of the lifestyle you want to maintain, per your vision, for the rest of your life.

The third and final bucket, which I call the PLUS bucket, will be funded with $500,000, which we know you will never need to use during your lifetime. The next question to ask yourself is *What do I want to do with this money?* Here are a few ideas: Use the PLUS money to fund gifts to children or grandchildren, make charitable contributions, convert some of your IRAs to a Roth IRA, purchase a second home, travel the world, or do whatever you desire. Because this money will be earmarked for different goals than those governing buckets one and two, which are dedicated to realizing the goal of living work-optionally, your investment strategy for the PLUS money will naturally be different from the strategy for the first two buckets. For example, if the money is being set aside for your children or grandchildren, you may want to be more aggressive with it, taking on greater risk for greater growth return.

Leaving a Legacy

Deciding what you will do with your PLUS bucket is an opportunity to take a step back and plan the legacy you want to leave for your own immediate family and even for multiple generations to come. There are many options, and the fundamental exercise of planning the PLUS bucket is always eye-opening for my clients. To gain an appreciation of the possibilities, let's go through the process in detail.

Here is an aspect of financial planning about which I have always felt strongly. You have worked and may still be working with all your heart, brains, and might for every single dollar you earn or have earned. You have built wealth, and you want to make sure your money stays in the bloodline. To reach this goal, it is important to maximize the greatest amount of your wealth for your loved ones—and to do so in a tax-efficient manner.

You must consider certain underlying factors. If you are married with children and have a family member whom you do not consider responsible when it comes to handling money, you must set up some parameters. Ask yourself this question: *If I suddenly died tomorrow, who would be inheriting my money? Do I feel comfortable with the answer?* Good estate planning gives you the ability to fully understand, while you are still alive and fully coherent, how to best transfer your wealth. Yet many people go through their lives without even the simplest form of estate planning. Please, please, please understand that if you do not have a clearly written will, a judge in a court system who knows nothing about your family dynamics will make all inheritance decisions for you. A high-priority action item is to speak with an estate attorney now if you have not already done so.

The objective of estate planning is to create knowledge, understanding, and a clearly drawn map showing exactly how you want your transfer of wealth to be carried out. These are the objectives:

- Document your intentions.
- Transfer assets to the people or trusts that *you* choose.
- Appoint a guardian to care for your children if you become incapacitated.
- Appoint a person to make medical decisions for you if you become incapacitated.
- If you wish to do so, provide charitable gifts to organizations you choose.
- Minimize potential expenses and taxes.
- Avoid legal and financial complications, as well as destructive family disputes.
- Transfer business interest according to a succession plan.
- Provide peace of mind for today and tomorrow.

This is the mission of planning for your estate while you are alive and able. The first and simplest part of estate planning is to complete these documents:

Will: This document provides instructions for the distribution of your estate upon your death and names an executor to administer your estate in accordance with the will.

Durable Power of Attorney: By this legal document, you (the "principal") appoint a person or persons ("attorney(s)-in-fact") to exercise the powers you enumerate. A *durable* power of attorney becomes effective when you become incapacitated (through illness or accident) such that you are no longer able to ensure that your finances are taken care of.

Health Care Proxy: This document appoints a person (health care agent) who can make healthcare decisions for you if you are unable to do so yourself.

Living Will: A living will documents your personal wishes concerning life support (being kept alive by medical means) under certain conditions, which may include chronic coma, persistent vegetative state, inability to communicate your needs, inability to recognize family or friends, total dependence on others for daily care, and other circumstances that you may choose to define.

The next step is to use your financial planning tools to assess the potential of a federal or state estate tax problem occurring at some point down the road. Laws change. At the time this book was written, the federal estate tax exemption for 2022 was $12.06 million per person. If your total net worth is less than this number upon your death, you will be exempted from federal estate tax. Here's the pertinent issue, however: in 2026, due to the Tax Cuts and Jobs Act of 2017 (TCJA), the federal estate tax exemption decreases to approximately $6.4 million. You may be under the $12.06 million today, but by 2026, when the exemption sunsets, you may be worth more than $6.4 million. Be aware and plan or modify your plan accordingly.

The next estate tax issue is the potential for *state* estate taxes. The laws vary from state to state. For example, where I live in New York, the estate tax exemption sits at $6.11 million for 2022. If your net worth is under $6.11 million, you will have no New York State estate taxes. Some states, such as Florida, have no estate taxes. Review the law as it exists in your state of legal residence. If you move to a different state, you may well need to alter your financial plan.

Dive Into the Analysis

Dive deeper into your financial analysis, and you may recognize that, at some point in the future, your estate may be worth more than the federal estate tax exemption of $12.06 million today or the $6.4 million in 2026. This is when you need to call on an estate-planning attorney, who can design a strategy to ensure that you maximize the wealth that will be transferred to your family. Understand that your total net worth today could be $9 million. If you are only fifty or sixty years old and live to be ninety-five, your estate will almost certainly be worth more than $9 million at some point before your death. This is why you need to do a planning analysis to understand where you are today so that you can predict where you could be in the future. The earlier you make a plan, the better.

Trusts

Once you complete your deep financial analysis, it's time to meet with an estate planning attorney. This is where you will learn about trusts and how they can be powerful tools for implementing the design of your estate plan. A trust is a legal entity that can be created to hold title to assets as well as manage and distribute them according to specific terms and conditions you can specify and customize. You will serve as the grantor, who creates the trust, names the trustees and the beneficiaries, and transfers assets or property to the trust. The trustee (who can be one or more parties) holds title to trust assets and administers the trust according to specified terms and conditions. The beneficiaries (who can be one or more parties) receive the benefits of the trust. These may include income or assets, according to the terms of the trust. The trust agreement is a legal document created by the grantor.

Establishing a trust has many benefits, including:

Avoiding probate, associated expenses, and publicity

Isolating and transferring assets, even if your will is contested

Distributing property among beneficiaries or equalizing inheritances

Simplifying the distribution of certain assets, such as property that you own

Reducing or eliminating potential federal and state estate taxes

Irrevocable vs Revocable Trusts

Irrevocable and revocable are the two main types of trusts. Revocable trusts allow you to revoke the agreement at any point. The main benefits of revocable trusts are that assets can be transferred in or out of the trust without any annual limitations, you can avoid probate upon demise, and your family can inherit the assets quicker than going through the court system.

Irrevocable trusts are primarily used to transfer assets out of one's estate to minimize federal and state estate taxes. For many people, the great drawback is that they lose control of those assets that are transferred into these types of trusts. On the one hand, you can potentially save your family estate taxes when you die. However, while you are alive, you lose control of the assets, which creates both financial and psychological complications. Another issue is that naming trustees to these trusts requires careful consideration because the trustee or trustees make decisions on the trust assets going forward. Trusting the trustee(s) can create another level of anxiety for the benefactor, one that often prevents people from taking this important step toward maximizing wealth by minimizing taxes.

Thinking About Your Legacy

The single most important takeaway from this chapter is that the time to think about your future and the future of your family is now. First, take the steps needed to educate yourself. Second, implement strategies to maximize the wealth that you have worked so hard to accrue. You want to set your wealth on a course that will serve your family for generations to come. Spend the time now to go through a detailed financial planning analysis to discover your net worth today, how it can potentially grow in the future, and what you can do to minimize federal and state estate taxes. Some of the richest families in the world have used trusts for many reasons other than what I have outlined here. For just about everyone, however, a major strategic consideration is to avoid taxes and make sure your money gets into the hands of the right family members.

Financial planning invites procrastination. Reject that invitation. Don't get hung up on the fear of what you may discover or fear of being overwhelmed by the amount of work it may take to find and sort through the necessary records. When it comes to planning for your legacy, procrastination can cost your loved ones many thousands, even millions, of dollars. Today is the day to start getting yourself organized and ready to roll.

CHAPTER 13

THE FINAL CUT: MINIMIZING TAXES

U nlocking a work-optional lifestyle is not just about the investment return you receive on your money year after year. In fact, the strategies you create and execute to minimize and defer your taxes are even more important than investment. If you take the time to create the right minimization strategies, you will position yourself to grow substantially more wealth over time. This is essential to ensuring that you don't run out of money before you run out of life.

Taxes affect virtually every aspect of your personal finances. As such, it behooves you to ask yourself if you are using tax laws to your advantage. These questions need to be asked and answered as you construct your overall financial strategy. There is an adage many financial planners love to invoke: *It's not what you make. It's what you keep.* This is not always easy, especially since tax law is subject to rapid change and evolution. It is not carved in stone, as this chart demonstrates.

Income **Taxes**

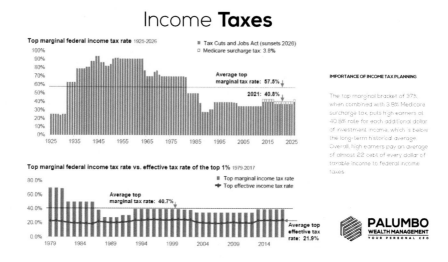

Begin by understanding how the federal income tax brackets work. As you can see in the chart, there are seven brackets in the 2022 federal income tax tables.

2022 Federal
Income Tax Tables

Married, filing jointly

Tax rate	Taxable income bracket	Tax owed
10%	$0 to $19,900	10% of taxable income
12%	$19,901 to $81,050	$1,990 plus 12% of the amount over $19,900
22%	$81,051 to $172,750	$9,328 plus 22% of the amount over $81,050
24%	$172,751 to $329,850	$29,502 plus 24% of the amount over $172,750
32%	$329,851 to $418,850	$67,206 plus 32% of the amount over $329,850
35%	$418,851 to $628,300	$95,686 plus 35% of the amount over $418,850
37%	$628,301 or more	$168,993.50 plus 37% of the amount over $628,300

Many people review their gross income and assume that the entire amount will be taxed within the bracket in which they file. As an example, if your gross income is $200,000, you may assume that your total tax bracket will be 24%. But because of the way the system is structured, your gross income must be reduced by various deductions, credits, and other adjustments. This reduces your taxable income amount, which, based on the set tables, is taxed at different marginal tax rates. You end up with a blended rate, called your effective tax rate, which is generally much lower than your marginal rate.

Once you have a basic understanding of how income tax works, you can begin thinking about two major strategies for managing it: *minimizing* taxes and *deferring* taxes. The chart shows that minimizing taxes can significantly reduce your returns while deferring your taxes has tremendous benefits for further maximizing your wealth over time.

Benefits of Deferring Taxes
Taxable vs. Tax Deferred Savings

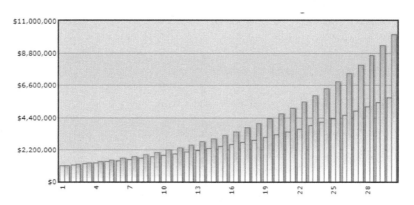

Learning How to Minimize and Defer

Review and understand your deductible expenses

Let's start with the concept of minimizing taxes. Consolidating deductible expenses, versus taking the standard deduction is one strategy for creating an optimum tax-reduction scheme. The objective is to reduce your gross income. You need to review and understand what deductions you can take that are greater than your standard deductions.

Examples of deductible expenses include mortgage interest and points, property taxes, state and local income taxes, and sales taxes. Other items that count are dental or medical work within the year's period that are not covered by insurance. Finally, charitable contributions also can be deducted. Instead of making one annual charitable contribution during the calendar year, think about breaking the contribution into two sums. Make one donation at the beginning of the year and one at the end of the year. Spending time with a tax accountant who can assist you in understanding what's deductible and what's not deductible can make a profound difference in how great a reduction you can make in your gross income.

Use the capital loss rules

The second gross income reduction strategy is to use the capital loss rules to your advantage. Capital losses—securities you sold for less than your purchase price—can also offset gains in taxable accounts. At a minimum, you will want to take advantage of the $3,000 in losses that the government allows to offset against earned income each year. Losses above $3,000 can also be carried forward to offset against future gains. This is important to understand as you review your personal portfolio. Throughout any given period, you will recognize that certain investments may perform poorly for the duration of that calendar year. In this case, you may be able to take a loss that you can use to offset against a future gain. Here's a great example of this. Bonds in the first quarter of 2022 went through one of their worst declines in history. Rather than stare at such losses and do nothing, you, as a savvy investor, sell some of your bonds laterally by moving them into other types of like-kind investments. Such "like-kind exchanges"—disposing of one asset and acquiring another similar asset—avoid generating a capital gains tax liability from the sale of the first asset. Like-kind exchanges put you in a position to avoid missing out on a potential investment upside even as you capture losses that can be used in the future. To cite another example, in March 2020, when the Covid-19 pandemic hit, the stock market rapidly declined, giving many people an opportunity to capture losses they could later use to offset future gains.

By pursuing this loss-capturing strategy over multiple years, you make a major positive impact on your wealth accumulation. Additionally, if you experience gains throughout the year, it is important to take the time to comb through your portfolio to see if there are any losses you can realize to offset your gains. When I was very young and first diving into the wealth management profession, a prospective client came into my office after attending one of my events. I asked him to bring his tax returns and brokerage statements for me to look over. When I saw the capital loss/gain column on his tax return, I noticed that he showed a $57,000 gain. I immediately looked at his brokerage statement, which showed unrealized losses of $125,000. His advisor could have used this number to significantly offset his current gains and even future gains. Because his financial advisor was not fully knowledgeable about taxes, however, his client paid approximately $20,000 in taxes he could have legitimately avoided.

You must make some assessment about where you feel the economy and market are going to go while you also study ways to reduce your taxes throughout the year. In strategically capturing losses, you do need to understand what the IRS calls the "wash-sale rule." This tax regulation prohibits selling an investment for a loss and replacing it with the same or "substantially identical" investment thirty days before or after the sale. For example, if you own XYZ mutual fund and you have an unrealized loss that you realize by selling it, you cannot buy that fund back for thirty-one days. If you do, the IRS will not allow you to use that loss to deduct against realized gains or to deduct from your tax return going forward. To avoid violating the wash-sale rule, you could sell the losing mutual fund and then move it into a different mutual fund with similar investments. If those investments rise over that thirty-day period, you can legally capture the gain. Of all the tax-reduction strategies we've discussed, capturing losses is one of the most effective, but people don't often take advantage of it. Why not? *Because they don't know about it!*

A third strategy you should put into action is minimizing or avoiding the use of mutual funds in taxable accounts. You might be a new investor in a mutual fund and not be aware that there is a large capital gain distribution on which you must pay taxes. If you've owned the mutual fund for a very short time, you might be down in terms of the investment yet still have to pay capital gains. As such, mutual funds are very tax-inefficient. Suppose, for example, that the fund has owned Microsoft for the past ten years when the portfolio manager, for whatever reason, decides to sell Microsoft after realizing its tremendous gains. Then, you come along and decide to purchase this mutual fund because of its track record. Guess what? You are responsible for paying taxes on this specific capital gain the portfolio recognized with Microsoft when you buy into the fund.

When you own single securities, such as single stocks or bonds instead of a managed portfolio, you have much more control over these types of situations. You are better able to determine what you want to sell or purchase while making certain that you are also doing all that you can to minimize taxes. With a mutual fund, you lose much of that control. Knowing this, if you still want to invest in mutual funds, you must inquire about any potential capital gain distributions that may occur. And you must do this *before* you buy into the fund. Understand that the representative you speak to may well be aware of what's going on today but perhaps does not know if the portfolio manager will decide to sell a long-term winner tomorrow. Again: I advise avoiding mutual funds. If you feel strongly about investing in them, however, at least minimize your exposure as much as possible.

A popular fourth tax reduction strategy involves charitable donations. If you are charitably inclined and over the age of seventy-two, you can use your required minimum distribution to fund a charitable donation. At this age, it becomes mandatory to start taking distributions from any IRA you have, and you must pay taxes at ordinary income rates. Instead of taking your distribution, depositing it in your checking account, and paying taxes, you are allowed to make a donation to a charitable organization *directly* from your IRA account. By doing this, you will not pay taxes on that distribution. I can't tell you how many times prospective clients, who later became long-term clients, made $30,000 to $50,000 in charitable donations by writing a check. If you have an IRA, are over the age of seventy-two, and want to save on taxation of your mandatory distributions, make your charitable donations directly. You are limited to a maximum of $100,000 in any given year, but this is an easy way to minimize taxes.

The fifth tax-minimizing strategy to consider is using the Step-Up in Cost Basis (also called the Step-Up in Basis). First, let me explain what this strange-sounding thing is.

When an inherited asset—such as real estate, stocks, and so on—are passed on after death, a Step-Up in Cost Basis provision in the IRS rules adjusts the value (the "cost basis") of the asset to its fair market value at the time of the benefactor's death. This often eliminates the capital gain that accrued between the original purchase of the asset and the heir's acquisition (that is, the date of the original owner's death). So, if you, as a potential benefactor, have an investment in a taxable account that has a low-cost basis—and you believe in the long-term value of that investment so that you intend to hold it—you must understand that when your beneficiaries inherit it, their cost basis will be the value of the asset on the date of your death. The heir receives a cost basis that (if the asset has grown in value since its purchase) effectively erases the capital gain by treating beneficiaries as if they had purchased the inherited asset on the date on which it transferred to them—that is, the date of the benefactor's death.

Let's examine the implications of this strategy more closely. If you acquire an asset with what you consider potential for long-term appreciation, you may want to earmark this specifically for your legacy. Many investors, however, make the big mistake of giving such an investment to their children and/or grandchildren while they are still alive. In doing so, the original cost basis, with its implication of hefty capital gains taxes, carries over to the family member. Indeed, when it comes to gifting your investments while you are living, it is imperative that you are fully cognizant of the Step-Up In Cost Basis concept. I remember talking to a prospective client about a situation in which his family had transferred ownership of their mother's house to a sibling. Their concern was that, if the mother needed long-term care, Medicaid could potentially come after their mother's home. She had purchased the property forty years earlier at a very low cost. By transferring ownership while the original purchaser was living, however, they transferred the low-cost basis to all potential heirs. The mother did end up needing long-term care for a short while before passing away. After her death, her children decided to sell the home. With a cost basis of $50,000, it sold for $950,000—wonderful appreciation, but they ended up having to pay taxes on $900,000, a total of $320,000. It was a liability that could easily have been avoided if they had a greater understanding of the applicable tax law. This is just one example of the many I've seen over the years, tax blunders that cost families thousands, even millions of dollars. With a little timely knowledge, such losses are wholly preventable.

Another situation to be aware of is when you share a joint account with an investment that has a low-cost basis. For instance, if your spouse has a terminal illness and the investment is moved from joint ownership to the spouse's name exclusively, the survivor will receive that investment with a new cost basis upon the death of the asset-owning spouse. In such a case, the cost basis is the value as of the date of death of the decedent. This timely transfer strategy can save the surviving spouse a great deal of money.

We turn now to a sixth strategy: Learn about tax-advantaged or tax-free income options. When you invest in real estate, specifically in multi-family properties, there are several tax benefits that you can receive. If you own multiple properties, you are considered a real estate investor and will be able to take the various deductions and depreciation that come from owning such properties. This can create a tax advantage income stream for you. As the value of your properties increases over time, you can sell them and purchase what is known as a "like-kind property," a property of the same character but perhaps of a different quality or grade. Doing this can defer the capital gains taxes on the sale of the original property.

Many billionaires have taken advantage of the tax benefits accorded to real estate investors under the like-kind rule and have grown their fortunes based on it. If you invest in private REITs (Real Estate Investment Trusts) or private credit that lends money to real estate investors, the income derived from those investments can also be tax-advantaged. The federal tax provision allows for a 20 percent deduction on pass-through income through the end of 2025. Individual-rate shareholders can deduct 20 percent of the taxable weekly dividend income that they receive (but not for dividends that qualify for capital-gain rates). In many cases, a portion of the dividend may be listed as a nontaxable return of capital. This can occur when the REIT cash distribution exceeds its earnings. An example is when the investment company takes large depreciation expenses. If this occurs, your cost basis will be reduced by the amount of the nontaxable portion of the dividend. Therefore, if you invested $1 million in a private REIT that pays 5 percent in income, this would equate to $50,000. If all this is nontaxable according to these rules, your new cost basis is $950,000, and the $50,000 in income is not taxable. So, when you sell your private REITs, you will be taxed on the difference of $1 million minus $950,000. Ideally, you want to defer this tax as long as you possibly can, unless you're unhappy about your investment or you need the money for some pressing reason.

Tax-free municipal bonds can also be used as a good alternative to corporate bonds in taxable accounts if you are in a high tax bracket. Historically, municipal bonds have a very low default rate and are considered more conservative than owning corporate bonds. As an example, you need to evaluate what a five-year investment-grade corporate bond would pay in interest, versus a five-year investment-grade municipal bond. When you factor in the after-tax return of the taxable corporate bond versus your tax-free income from the municipal bond, you will understand which investment offers the greater benefit on an after-tax basis. In evaluating corporate versus municipal bond investment, you must ask your accountant, who knows your marginal tax rate, to carry out this analysis and confirm which is the better investment for you. Often, I see investors who fail to put in the time required for this evaluative comparison. They end up investing in taxable corporate bonds, which are much riskier and, on an after-tax basis, not as tax-advantaged as municipal bonds.

Deferring Taxes

Deferring your taxes is another powerful way to compound wealth over time. As you can see in the tax chart included at the beginning of this chapter, there is, over time, a tremendous difference between a taxable account that pays taxes on an ongoing basis versus a tax-deferred account that first taxes on an annual basis. The key is to understand how you can benefit from the deferred option.

The first deferment strategy is simply to participate in your employer's employer-sponsored retirement plan. If you are a business owner, put a high priority on setting up a retirement plan for you and your employees. Familiar employer-sponsored plan examples are the 401(k), 403B, 457, SEP IRA, and defined-benefit plans. These all allow you to contribute pretax dollars, which reduces your overall taxable income. For example, if you make $200,000 per year and you're under fifty years old, you can contribute up to $20,500, deferring payment of taxes on that amount of your income. If you're over fifty, you can contribute an additional $6,500 per year. If your gross income is $200,000 and you have contributed $20,500 to your 401(k), your new gross income is $179,500. You benefit by reducing your overall gross income by contributing $20,500 to a 401(k), which will grow tax-deferred until you must take the money out at seventy-two. If you are the owner of a business that shows a consistent profit, you can set up a defined benefit plan that allows you to contribute up to $245,000 a year (as of 2022).

There are many details to understand, but employer-sponsored retirement plans could become a tremendous saving opportunity that also offers the benefits of deferring a large sum of taxable money over time. If you do not have access to an employer-sponsored plan, you can invest in an IRA, which could potentially become deductible based on how much income you earn. The more you earn, the less the deductibility of the IRA. A Roth IRA is another great option for the deferment of taxes. Your contributions to the Roth IRA are not tax deductible, but your account grows tax-deferred, just as it does with an IRA. The key difference between an IRA and a Roth IRA is that the Roth does not oblige you to take out mandatory distributions at age seventy-two. Even more important, any distributions you do take out in the future are tax-free, whereas IRA distributions are fully taxable.

Both IRAs and Roth IRAs are among the most powerful retirement vehicles available, especially for legacy planning, which we will discuss in greater detail shortly. Each of these retirement vehicles will allow you to contribute a set amount. If you're under fifty, you can put in $6,000 per year, and if you're over fifty, you can put in $7,000 per year.

The second deferment strategy is called a "backdoor Roth IRA conversion." If you are a high-income earner who is maximizing your employer-sponsored retirement plan and/or you are a business owner contributing to your own retirement plan, you can contribute to an IRA that is non-tax-deductible if you make too much money. This can be immediately converted to a Roth IRA. For example, if a husband-and-wife duo does not have an IRA set up, and they made too much money to be able to contribute to an IRA and receive the backdoor Roth IRA conversion is a workaround option. Assuming this couple is under fifty years old, they can contribute $6,000 each to their IRA and again, not get the deduction but immediately move that money into a Roth IRA. If you apply some math and you execute this properly over a twenty-year period at a 6 percent rate of return, the combined growth of these two accounts could be $467,912, possibly tax-free, if the couple follows the suggested steps and takes withdrawals. Alternatively, when the beneficiaries inherit these funds, the accounts receivable end will also be tax-free.

The third IRA/Roth IRA strategy is to review the benefits of converting your IRA, or even just part of your IRA, to a Roth IRA. I previously introduced this concept of your *plus money*, the money you will never need to use over your lifetime. As an example, assume a married couple who has $2 million in taxable accounts and $2 million in retirement accounts. Let's also assume that they need $3.5 million of that money to live their life's vision. That leaves $500,000 in *plus money*, which they can plan on using to implement a legacy strategy. Their next step is to do an analysis of converting $500,000 of the $2 million that is in IRAs into a Roth IRA. The downside of this is having to pay taxes on the full $500,000 that you are converting. The right time to execute this transfer is during a period when you believe that your income level is lower than normal. If you've taken a loss—perhaps from a business opportunity that didn't work out—take advantage of it by converting the $500,000 now. It is the perfect time. The actual process typically unfolds over multiple years, which reduces the amount of taxes that you will have to pay on an annual basis. (You *can* convert the entire $500,000 in one year if for some reason you want to do this. In such a case, be certain to pay the taxes with taxable money. Do not take it out of the $500,000 you are converting to a Roth IRA.)

Most people will want to make the conversion over a period of years. You should run an analysis based on the benefits of converting over a ten, twenty, or thirty-year period. By doing the analysis this way, you will be able to see the benefits of that option versus leaving the full $2 million in your IRA, knowing that you will have required taxable distributions at seventy-two years old. When you do a side-by-side analysis of leaving the $2 million in the IRA versus having $1.5 million in IRAs and $500,000 in the Roth IRAs, you will see that there is a significant difference in after-tax value versus not converting to a Roth IRA.

This may all look great on paper, but the pushback I often hear from my clients is that they do not want to take on the burden of paying extra taxes for something that is more beneficial for their heirs than for themselves in the here and now. Understandably, many of my clients want to reap more of the benefits of their wealth while they are still around to enjoy them. This is exactly why it is so crucial to understanding what is most important to you individually. For example, if you tell me that legacy planning and the transfer of your wealth to your family members are of paramount importance to you, then we will design a strategy like the one I just laid out. If instead you want to enjoy your life during its closing chapters by using your funds to the maximum and leaving to your children only what fraction remains, we will devise another plan. This is a very personal decision that, in the end, only you can make. The great mistake is trying to compare yourself and your situation to what other people are doing.

There is a fourth deferment strategy for legacy planning, which calls for educating your beneficiaries about the benefits of stretching out your IRA, which they may later inherit. For example, let's assume you have an IRA valued at $1 million and you have a child or two children who are irresponsible when it comes to money. If you pass away, your children will have a few choices to make. They can defer paying any taxes for ten years if they leave your IRA intact, or they take a lump sum with taxes paid in full for that particular year. If one of your children decides to do this, they could be liable for up to $500,000 in taxes. This is a terrible waste of money, which is why you must educate your children on topics of money and the potential inheritances that they may receive.

The fifth deferment strategy involves taking asset distributions. If you are in a life phase where you are receiving distributions from your accounts, it is imperative that you draw them from the most tax-efficient account. If you have $2 million in a taxable account, $2 million in a retirement account, and you are taking a 4 percent withdrawal from the total value of both these accounts (which equals hundred $160,000), you should take the money from the taxable accounts if you're under seventy-two years old. By doing so, you allow the value of your retirement account to continue growing while tax-deferred.

We have already introduced—in another context—the sixth strategy in this chapter, which is to invest part of your portfolio in real estate. When the value of your properties increases and you sell them, you can invest the proceeds in a like-kind property. Called a 1031 exchange, this type of transaction allows you to defer your taxes. Typically, real estate investors start out small and then, over multiple years, sell two or three properties, and 1031 exchange into a larger property, and continue to defer the taxes over multiple years or multiple generations.

Many multi-billionaire real estate investors today took many years and more than a few generations to get to the point where they are now. Think about all those deferrals of taxes that occurred throughout those years. We are talking about millions of dollars in tax savings.

The strategies I have laid out in this chapter are among the most important ways to minimize taxes on an annual basis. Done right, minimizing taxes amounts to maximizing wealth over time. The first question new clients *always* ask me is: What *rate of return will you be able to achieve with my money?*

Of course, that touches on an important aspect of how I serve my clients, but it is a question that should be accompanied by another: *How will you assist me in minimizing taxes and reducing risk?*

Here's the answer. There are four main ways to compound your wealth over time: achieve a respectable rate of return, minimize fees and commissions, minimize taxes and defer taxes, and minimize downside risk. All four of these are equally important because each contributes to the goal of maximizing your wealth in the long run. As you think about the notion of unlocking a work-optional lifestyle for yourself, these four components must play a leading role in successfully achieving your goal for you and your family.

To Sum Up

Drawing on more than two decades of work in wealth management, I have presented you with a distillation of all that I learned. I have written each chapter to assist you along your journey by providing the tools and knowledge that will maximize your money and put you in a position where you can enjoy your money rather than worry about it. If you follow my guidance here, I believe you will reach a point where work is optional and you have the time to live out your own life's true vision.

Here are the key takeaways from this book:

Not worrying about your money starts with understanding your vision for your life now and in the future.

Take time to understand what your lifestyle costs will be if you live to be ninety-five years old.

Build a financial plan and go through repeated analyses of how much money you need to have saved, what rate of return you need, and how much risk you are willing to take on. Thus framed, these analyses will reveal to you what cash flow you need to make work optional.

Invest your money based on free cash flow.

Balance your portfolio properly by using asset classes that have low to negative correlation with stocks. This helps you to protect your capital during difficult economic periods.

Rebalance by continuously reviewing your investments and making sure they are not overvalued. If they are, consider reducing your exposure and repositioning the proceeds to the parts of your portfolio that are undervalued.

Become a student of the markets by reading as many books as possible and watching videos about the best investors in the world— the likes of Warren Buffett, Charlie Munger, and Ray Dalio, and model yourself after them.

Have an advanced planning strategy that includes continually working to find new ways to mitigate taxes, transfer your assets efficiently to your loved ones, protect your estate from lawsuits and unforeseen illnesses, understand your family dynamics, and magnify gifts to charities.

You work hard for every dollar you earn; therefore, respect EVERY DOLLAR YOU EARN! Understand that, if managed correctly, each of those dollars will contribute to setting you up for an incredible lifestyle that will endure through the rest of your life. You can do it. Believe me when I say that. Use this book as a foundation to teach you how to think about your money and your future. With discipline, diligence, and a reasonable portion of good luck, you *will* get to the point where work is optional and achieve financial peace of mind. NOW, JUST DO IT!

Appendix A

The Power of Compounding: Better Understanding the Upside of Long-Term Investing

Most individuals know that compounding investment returns (continually reinvesting) can be helpful to their long-term investment results, but few understand the dynamics of the math behind it. Relatively insignificant amounts of money, invested regularly, over a long period of time can result in a more significant savings pool than one might otherwise realize.

This appendix sets out to help investors understand the value of compounding returns over a "longer-term investment horizon," such as when you are investing for the proverbial "retirement." In doing so, they carefully analyze the downside, which is appropriate. Yet few advisors explain the potential upsides, albeit with the appropriate caveats of "Past returns do not guarantee future outcomes". But it is important to understand the upside and the power of compounding when thinking about your savings and investment strategy and how it could accelerate your ability to reach your "Make Work Optional" goal!

We start by providing examples to demonstrate the potential investment outcomes by changing the inputs: the upfront capital, the monthly contributions, and the overall investment return. Here are the important lessons to remember:

- Starting a savings program early is extremely helpful, even with very modest capital.
- Adding to that savings consistently is extremely helpful, again, even with very modest capital.
- Not surprisingly, the rate of return level is the most impactful, followed by monthly contributions and upfront capital.

Palumbo Wealth Management (PWM) demonstrates these concepts through PWM's *OnePlan* planning exercise with our clients as we discuss their overall financial plan for achieving "peace of mind" in their senior years. We seek to explain to our clients the following range of results based on the level of acceptable risk with which they are comfortable:

- The potential long-term risk of "inadequate capital growth" and a loss of purchasing power resulting from the unwillingness to assume short-term portfolio volatility and the associated drawdowns.
- The potential for adequate capital growth and an increase in purchasing power resulting from assuming moderate short-term portfolio volatility and market drawdowns with the objective of achieving higher capital returns.

For most everyone, it is uncomfortable to assume "higher risk" in their investment portfolio. We would all be comfortable never making an investment that goes down in value. However, at Palumbo Wealth Management, we believe it is important that each investor understands both the potential downside as well as the upside of assuming investment risk prior to making any portfolio decisions. In concert with our team, we seek to educate our clients on the "return/risk" tradeoff and target attractive risk-adjusted returns that enable you to achieve peace of mind with your investment program.

The first priority of investment savings is to maintain purchasing power versus inflation.

Entering into almost any investment strategy that seeks to maintain purchasing power will require the assumption of market risk with the hope of increased valuations over longer periods of time. Investing in very low-risk investments over time may not be adequate to keep pace with inflation, especially when tax effects are factored in. The result would be a loss of purchasing power, and thus a diminished lifestyle.

Below we demonstrate examples that show the effects on capital growth by changing:

- Monthly contributions
- Up-front dollar amounts and
- Increasing the targeted rate of returns
- Doubling your investment horizon from 20 to 40 years
1. The value of increasing monthly contributions over 20 or 40 years versus a higher upfront dollar commitment

a. A $100 increase in the monthly contribution to $300 is more valuable than doubling the upfront money from $2,500 to $5,000.

2. The non-linear increase in the resulting dollars by raising the monthly compound return:

a. Increasing the return to 7.5% is more valuable than doubling the contribution to $400 a month.

b. Increasing the return to 15% annually from 5% over 20 years results in almost 4 times the assets.

3. In all cases, doubling the horizon to 40 years from 20 years much more than doubles the resulting outcome, regardless of return or contribution, making the case for starting an investment plan as early as you can.

Investing over 20 Years					
Upfront and Monthly	5%	7.5%	10%	12.5%	15%
$2,500 initial, $200 per month	$88,988	$121,898	$170,193	$241,763	$348,736
$5,000 initial, $200 per month	$95,969	$133,050	$188,514	$271,829	$398,025
$10,000 initial, $200 per month	$109,333	$155,354	$225,155	$331,959	$496,603
$50,000 initial, no contributions	$135,632	$223,041	$366,404	$601,299	$985,775
$2,500 initial, $300 per month	$130,091	$177,271	$246,131	$347,613	$498,461
$2,500 initial, $400 per month	$171,195	$232,644	$322,068	$453,462	$648,185
$2,500 initial, $500 per month	$212,298	$288,017	$398,005	$558,312	$797,909

Investing over 40 Years					
Upfront and Monthly	5%	7.5%	10%	12.5%	15%
$2,500 initial, $200 per month	$323,600	$654,512	$1,399,067	$3,199,142	$7,174,960
$5,000 initial, $200 per month	$341,996	$704,259	$2,165,727	$3,480,703	$8,146,714
$10,000 initial, $200 per month	$378,788	$704,259	$1,533,319	$3,480,703	$8,146,714
$50,000 initial, no contributions	$367,921	$994,944	$2,685,033	$7,231,204	$19,435,034
$2,500 initial, $300 per month	$476,202	$956,894	$2,031,475	$4,497,934	$10,276,568
$2,500 initial, $400 per month	$628,804	$1,259,276	$2,663,883	$5,876,725	$13,378,174
$2,500 initial, $500 per month	$781,406	$1,561,658	$3,296,292	$7,255,516	$16,479,779

Past performance does not guarantee future returns. These scenarios are meant as an education to understand the power of compounding and on-going contributions in investing. Base case in bold. Calculated using www.Investor.gov Compound Interest Calculator. *Compounded Monthly with monthly contributions over 20 and 40 years with no withdrawals, no taxes. **Base case in bold**

While some investors may not feel comfortable with a 20-year investment horizon, with the average person living well into their 70's, the 20-year horizon is certainly an appropriate period for most investors, including those in their 60s and 70s. The 40-year horizon is certainly appropriate for those in their 40's and younger. When planning investments, the analysis should be conservative, expecting a longer life to assure adequate funds.

I hope this Appendix offers a clearer perspective and understanding of the power of investment horizon, regular savings, and selected return targets for all investors.

- Regular contributions to savings, even small dollar amounts, are valuable and become more so as the investment horizon expands.
- The earlier you start saving the better!
- Better understanding the risk and return trade-off can be helpful in deciding risk tolerance in long-term planning.

Understanding the concepts outlined here is critical to those millennials saving for retirement as well as those setting aside assets for young children and the next generation. A more informed perspective is valuable as investors decide when and how much to save for the long-term.

Every investor needs to assess investments they make based on their personal risk tolerance, however being informed about the potential effects of such decisions is equally important.

Disclosures:

Past performance is not a guarantee of future returns. This chart is not meant to imply or suggest that any return level is achievable over any type of investment horizon. It is simply seeking to demonstrate the sensitivities to capital growth based on upfront investment capital, ongoing contributions, and the target rate of return over both 20 and 40 years. This also demonstrates the value of starting investment plans as early as possible.

Future asset levels based on were calculated at

https://www.investor.gov/financial-tools-calculators/calculators/compound-interest-calculator.

Asset calculations are based on entering the required data, including a set starting dollar amount, a compounding rate (i.e., interest rate or return), selecting monthly compounding as well as a fixed monthly contribution over 20 and 40 years. The Calculator then generates a dollar figure, which is entered into the above chart.

ABOUT THE AUTHOR

Philip G. Palumbo is Founder, CEO and Chief Investment Officer of Palumbo Wealth Management. He is a contributor on CNBC, Bloomberg, Reuters, and TD Ameritrade Network. His market insights have been quoted in such leading publications as The Wall Street Journal and Barron's. He has authored, Make Work Optional, a book dedicated to assisting individuals and families on how to properly plan and invest their money. He served as Senior Vice President and Senior Portfolio Manager at UBS before forming Palumbo Wealth Management, a full-service boutique wealth management firm. Over the past 20 years, Philip has held senior roles with several major financial institutions and he has successfully assisted families and individuals navigate some of the most challenging market environments in recent history. The leadership Philip provided for his clients during these difficult markets has helped them achieve their most important financial goals as they prepare for retirement.

Philip's UBS practice, the Palumbo Wealth Management Group, was a premiere Long Island-based wealth management team. He has lectured and taught several hundred families and individuals throughout his career at a major university on subjects such as retirement and investment planning, tax, estate and trust planning, family governance and asset protection.

Philip has long held a tremendous inner passion for delivering exceptional financial advice and guidance to his clients and always putting their interest first before anyone else, no matter what. He has always felt that the way financial institutions deliver wealth management can be greatly improved. For this reason, Philip registered Palumbo Wealth Management as a Registered Investment Advisor. His vision was to create an environment where the only focus was on what is best for their clients.

Philip wants clients to know that the Palumbo Wealth Management serves as legal fiduciaries on every piece of advice it gives them and the firm has unlimited access to the best in breed products, services and research that are available within the financial services industry. Palumbo Wealth Management isn't just focused on profits, but rather on delivering an incredible world class experience and service offerings that would make clients proud.

As the firm's Chief Investment Officer, Philip has spent countless hours researching the changing economic environments and how various investment categories have performed over a 50 plus year time period. His findings from this research are the foundation to the investment models he utilizes to assist his clients in achieving their financial goals. Philip has 23 years of experience managing money over some of the most difficult and volatile market periods in history and he has used this experience and research to guide his clients effectively in achieving their financial goals.

Philip feels we all get one chance at life. Putting your best self forward and doing what you feel is right based on your core values and beliefs systems, is the WHY behind forming Palumbo Wealth Management.

Philip has earned the CERTIFIED FINANCIAL PLANNER™ (CFP®) designation. This designation is awarded to individuals who complete two years of specialized education, pass a comprehensive two-day examination, have required experience and meet ethical and continuing education requirements. Topics covered include retirement planning, insurance, employee-benefit planning, income planning, estate and trust planning, tax planning and investment strategies.

Philip received his B.A. in finance from Towson University where he played Division I Lacrosse. He resides in Manhasset, New York with his wife Melissa and their three sons, Philip, Andrew and Matthew. In his free time, Philip has a deep passion for coaching his three boys' lacrosse teams, reading investment books, weight training, playing golf and most importantly, spending time with his family.

Certified Financial Planner Board of Standards, Inc. (CFP Board) owns the certification marks CFP®, CERTIFIED FINANCIAL PLANNER™, CFP® (with plaque design), and CFP® (with flame design) in the U.S., which it authorizes use of by individuals who successfully complete CFP Board's initial and ongoing certification requirements.